Reclaiming Self-Worth:

The Five-Step Method to Releasing Limiting Beliefs
and Feeling Worthy

Suzanne McColl

Green Heart Living Press

Reclaiming Self-Worth: The Five-Step Method to
Releasing Limiting Beliefs and Feeling Worthy
Copyright © 2022 Suzanne McColl

ISBN Paperback: 978-1-954493-32-2

Cover design: Barb Pritchard

Dedication

To my clients who were brave, trusting, and courageous enough to allow themselves the gift of taking this self-reclamation journey, and who allowed me to be their guide in their often painful and scary journeys. They taught me about the resiliency of the human spirit, about the beauty of the process of healing, and of finding oneself.
They taught me about
the true meaning and purpose of life.

To my children whom I'm watching grow into confident, courageous, and loving humans. I have been blessed in also guiding them to the best of my abilities. They teach me to be humble,
to be compassionate, to take risks,
and to love and feel connected.
They also have shown me that we all have inherent worth as human beings.

What better lessons are there to learn in life?

Table of Contents

Introduction

My experiences as a psychotherapist for over 30 years have allowed me to accompany hundreds of clients on their journeys. Although they may all have different outcomes they are hoping to achieve in the process, I have synthesized it into one organizing category: Self-Worth.

Regardless of the area they are focusing on, the outcome they desire is always that they reclaim their self-worth. I say "reclaim" because I have come to believe that there is a part of us that is at our core that knows our self-worth. It is there from the beginning of our lives and perhaps that is the part of us that is really suffering because it is not being acknowledged, expressed, and set free. I believe we all have the capacity to reclaim our self-worth and it's a matter of learning a language that describes and guides us in evolving and healing.

From my experience, many of my clients have tried it all: positive affirmations, cognitive strategies, talk therapy, reading self-help books, listening to podcasts, and coaching. This may be you and you may have seen some progress but are still experiencing habitual negative beliefs about yourself that carry with them emotional distress.

My purpose in writing this book is to help you see that you already have everything you need, you just need a little guidance to see beyond the limiting beliefs you have been living with and unlock your potential.

Until we resolve our limiting beliefs, we can't fully leverage all we've learned to make lasting changes in our life.

Affirmations, talk therapy, and podcasts are great, but they don't tap into your neural pathways and release past emotional distress.

That's why I have written this book, grounded in the therapeutic practice of EMDR Therapy (Eye Movement and Desensitization and Reprocessing Therapy), which targets these limiting beliefs and allows you to resolve them once and for all. The quotes and stories from clients in this book are all from my clients with whom I have conducted EMDR therapy. Their transformations are from the result of learning how to view themselves and their feelings of worth from the perspectives I will be talking about in this book. EMDR therapy took them deeply into their inner worlds and created lasting changes in their perspectives on their own self-worth and on what is possible for them. But the perspective of understanding yourself from the viewpoint of the beliefs you hold about yourself that arise from the relationships and events in your life is the foundation upon which all change is possible.

This perspective can help you see what is holding you back from feeling good in your life and how to finally break through to greater peace, empowerment, and self-worth.

I was raised in upstate New York in a large family. I was the second of seven children. My parents were professionals and they were, as you can imagine, extremely busy. I had to do a lot of finagling to get my needs met in my family by being the "helper" and the "good child". I was the one who didn't cause any problems. I was "sweet". I remember my father stressing that I should smile a lot. That persona continued throughout my life in different ways. I was quiet in school and held back a lot in the early years of my professional life.

As a result of that, I didn't fully explore who I really was. When I was young my parents were focusing on keeping the family "machine" running. I didn't have an opportunity to have a lot of ongoing dialogue with my parents. It's that dialogue that's what's really helpful when it comes to getting to know yourself, and developing your personality. My personality development was more focused on the outside, on becoming who I thought was acceptable to other people.

What happened as a result of that was that I drew some conclusions about myself and my worth that made sense to me. I developed limiting beliefs that I wasn't important. *I'm not really enough.* My way of understanding things at the time was that I felt like I had to help other people in order to be enough. That was something I struggled with a lot. I thought I wasn't very smart or didn't have much to say. I believed I wasn't very interesting. As I continued to go through life - through school, college and in my adult career as a psychotherapist, I was good at what I did, but I was uncomfortable being outspoken. Public speaking was very hard for me.

I continually was trying to find ways to grow and to feel better about myself. I explored several kinds of therapy and energy work. This exploration led me into the world of Eye Movement Desensitization and Reprocessing therapy, which is all about resolving your limiting beliefs, resolving emotional distress from past experiences and allowing you to feel good about yourself. The more I resolved my own limiting beliefs, the freer I felt to follow my dreams.

In this book I am sharing with you the five-step BUILD method I've developed based on my own experience and working with hundreds of clients. This method will help you to change these life-long patterns, freeing yourself from the nagging sense that you are meant for more, that you are meant for something greater. It can help you to reclaim your self-worth, and build a life in alignment with this new awareness.

The Five-Step BUILD Method

1) **B - Believe** in your worth.

2) **U -Understand** the way we develop our sense of self and beliefs about ourselves.

3) **I - Identify** your limiting beliefs that are interfering with you owning your self-worth and how trauma may be having an impact on you.

4) **L- Learn** strategies, tools; educate yourself about emotional intelligence.

5) **D- Do**, practice all you've learned. Put it into action.

I'm going to be giving you educational information that you will be able to use to have a new way of looking at your life. You'll be learning what limiting beliefs are, how to understand yours, and where they came from. You will learn some strategies to be able to work with those so that you can let them go - and develop more positive attitudes about yourself in your life.

I will also be taking you through some exercises that will help you to bring in new internal coping resources. As you practice these strategies and visualization tools, you are going to be developing new neural pathways and tapping into some that you have already that you're just not using.

This book is arranged in such a way as to first, develop a cognitive awareness of everything you're struggling with. Then the experiential component will help you to have a better awareness of what your signals are on a physical level, as well as to develop more awareness of what the emotions are that might not have been processed. The exercises give you tools to work on letting go of your antiquated limiting beliefs.

Finally, in this book are the stories and quotes from clients with whom I've completed EMDR therapy. You will hear from them, what their struggles were in life and how they were able to transform and find their self worth. I am grateful for their willingness to share their stories with you in this book so that you could learn from their experiences. Their words are very powerful and, in my mind, they tell the stories of resilience and of the miracles of being human. That we can go from feeling lost and hopeless and transform to a place of self-worth, alignment and a place of hope. I hope that when you read their stories you allow yourself to see yourself in some of them and to see that you too can transform and find your self-worth again.

How to Get the Most out of this Book

My suggestion is that you read each section of the book and then pick up your journal and take some time to record your thoughts, feelings, and memories that may have arisen while reading the previous chapter. Begin to notice what comes up when you think about each section. Notice your limiting beliefs and where you might have gotten them in your life. Notice the emotional level that you've been experiencing in regards to yourself, others, as a result of past and current events. Pay attention to how you've been coping with these emotions. Notice where you might need to use some of the tools that we're talking about here in your everyday life. Take your time and try to integrate everything that you're learning as you go.

You may not understand everything as you are learning it for the first time. You can always go back and reread sections. Each time you read it, you may hear it in a different way and you may get something different out of it. That's kind of how life is. Life is a journey. We have to be compassionate toward ourselves and allow ourselves to take things in and learn at our own pace.

My understanding of life is that we are basically running a marathon, not sprinting. Along the way, there are a lot of twists and turns. We are presented with challenges. Show yourself compassion. If you have to put the book down for a little while, that's okay, you can come back to it.

This book is a means to an exploration of your life. You're going to be diving deep and looking at things in a different way than you usually do. In this process you may have different memories or feelings that come up that are not necessarily always easy to deal with.

Practice self-compassion and loving kindness. Those are terms that come from Buddhist philosophy and they're extremely important for all of us. Practice lots of self-care. Use this time as personal exploration time, almost like a self-guided retreat.

Get plenty of sleep because a lot of processing happens when you're sleeping. That's how EMDR got started, with the idea that the rapid eye movements that you have when you're sleeping help you to process the upsetting events in your lives. That is what will happen as you read this book and explore your own life circumstances. You may read some of this book and do some journaling and then at night when you're sleeping, your subconscious will continue processing the information.

Drink a lot of water. This kind of learning or any kind of personal growth is about tapping into energy in your body. With new understandings and new beliefs that you adopt, there's a lot of energy shifting going on and that means that your body is working hard. (Important concept: if there is emotional work going on, there is also work happening on a physical level. It's all connected.) In my experience as a therapist with my clients, they can feel drained when doing this kind of work and can get dehydrated. Staying hydrated helps.

Notice your negative self-talk. Try to switch it to something positive and even start your day out with writing down one to three positive affirmations about yourself and try to refer to them or put them somewhere maybe where you'll see them visually - on your laptop, your refrigerator or your mirror in the bathroom. Try to repeat them to yourself throughout the day.

Section I

Believe

"I wish I had known that there was hope, life would not always be gloomy. I wish I had appreciated my special people more and let them know how special they were to me. I wish I knew that I had a purpose or a multitude of purposes, a self-pride." - Client

(I wish I had known) I had permission to be human. Not everything was my fault. Somewhere along the way I was programmed for that." - Client

Chapter 1

How Our Beliefs Shape Our Experience

What if you had known all along in your life that you are worthy as a human being? What if you had known that as your birthright as a human being you are worthy and that you had that lens of worthiness to interpret everything in your life from that perspective?

When I work with my clients doing trauma resolution therapy, each client inevitably comes to a place where they step back, observe their lives from a newfound perspective of self-worth, and say, "Wow, I wish I had known this back then." There is a period of grieving what could have been. After they process that, they go on to create a life built upon a deep knowing of their self-worth.

Here are some of the thoughts that my clients have shared with me about what they wish they had known:

"I wish I would have found other people who were similar to me. I often had feelings of impending doom and I was certain I would die at a young age. I wish I had figured out where those emotions stemmed from earlier."

"I wish I had known that I am capable of handling myself in many different situations and that I should have no fear."

"I wish I understood that if my feelings were telling me someone is manipulating me, I'd have gone with it. I lived a life of shame that I didn't need to. For example, my sister was so cruel and degrading to me when I was young. When I complained she'd say I was a whiny baby. When I was 15 her husband used to sneak into my room and molest me. When I complained and told him to stop he told me I was a whiny baby. I let people get away with hurting me and ended up feeling shame because I complained about my mistreatment. Then I would feel the shame and pain of what they did. So many people did awful things to me. I let them. I wish I had self-worth. I wish I knew my gut was right. Granted I wasn't a perfect person...far from it, but I in no way deserved the abuse I received over my lifetime. I wish I knew this as a child."

"I wish I knew that the messages I received as a child did not need to define me. I wish I had known that it would have been ok to reach out to other adults/caring people for what I needed. I wish that I had known that I could have taken my feelings and thoughts seriously and that they were valid and deserved attention instead of dismissing them."

"I wish I had learned it was ok to make mistakes, that one can learn to let things go, to not always second guess myself. I wish I learned to understand grief and anticipatory grief."

(I wish I had known) "that it wasn't my fault. I was too young to make the decisions I did."

(I wish I had known) "that I had a mother who had psychiatric issues. I would have generated some comp-assion."

"This question brings tears to my eyes and an ache to my heart. I have lived virtually my whole life trying to wash myself clean from the shame and feelings of being a dirty little girl that came from being sexually assaulted by my grandfather. I wish I had known that it wasn't my fault. That I was an innocent little four-year-old girl who deserved to be protected, cherished, (and) allowed to be a child who felt safe and worthy. It would have prevented me from being further abused throughout my life because I would have known better! I would have known that I was worthy of receiving unconditional love. The good news is that I now know."

"I wish I had known that I am not responsible for what happened to me or to others around me that I love. I wish I and my caregivers had known that I am an empath and absorb feelings and energy of people around me. I wish I had known how deeply I feel and how it is a normal human reaction to emote. I wish I had known the questions to ask and the tools to process what I was feeling. I wish I had known that I am an introvert. I wish I had known that I can take time-outs to protect myself. I wish I had known that even if other people make decisions for me, I still have choices and should listen to my intuition. I wish I had known what intergenerational trauma is and the methods for coping with it. I wish I had known the true power that I have as a woman. I wish I had known that my mind isn't the only voice and that my heart and body are worth listening to as well. I wish I had known that I am loved and I am not alone."

"I wish I had known...how deeply ingrained my feelings of impossible responsibility for others had been developed, as a coping mechanism for self-worth as a child. And how that limited a healthy focus on my own life whenever crises arose."

"I wish I had known that people you hope you can trust to guide you can give you bad advice and can try to manipulate you into what they would like you to do/feel - whether this is conscious or not. Everyone should be assigned a clinical therapist at birth - things would be better. Advice would not be skewed to what the adult/parent/power person would like you to do."

"I wish I understood the red flags that are so obvious to me now around Narcissistic Personality Disorder. I wish I had known better how to balance the needs of others with my own needs. I wish I had had the confidence to sometimes put myself before others and to feel comfortable making a decision without fear and insecurity. I wish I had known the difference between looking within to understand my part in any situation and allowing others to use this personality trait to manipulate my confidence and understanding of situations."

"I wish I had known...that the adults in your life are struggling and push their desires and needs upon the children sometimes unintentionally or intentionally. The other thing is that I am an empath that I didn't have control over how people's feelings affected me - that I wasn't overreacting or over emotional."

"I wish I had known...that what I witnessed, felt, and experienced was as it seemed, and that the religious brain-

washing and gaslighting were just that - not truth. And that I would find true love and have a family."

"I wish I had known...that some of the things my parents told/influenced me about myself, weren't true. That I was worthwhile, strong, intelligent, a lovable person, and the only one I need to convince of this is me, not them or others."

"I wish I had known that at the end of the day the most important thing is feeling good about myself and staying true to who I am when it comes to making important decisions would make a world of difference. I don't think I could have understood those concepts when I was younger though. I also wish I knew when my family said they'd always be there, they meant it. Our relationship ebbed and flowed in so many ways and it remains the best part of all of this for me. Being depressed, I don't always want to be here, they make me stay. That's a gift I now have. I'm very grateful to them."

"I am an abused child and was also neglected. I started seeing a psychiatrist when I was 30 but I wish that I had started that journey earlier. I would have been able to do so much more with my life because mental health counseling would have given me the self-confidence that I needed. I would not have been so afraid and anxious. I would have had a much higher self-esteem. At present, I am 64 years old and I own my own house, have a lot of friends, a social network, a great boyfriend, and a really well-paying job. So...successful by some standards. A very long way from the way I started my life. I have worked hard to get here but I know I could have accomplished so much more and would have had significantly less fear and

anxiety if I had mental health counseling earlier in my life."

As you were reading these thoughts from people you don't know, perhaps the sentiments resonate with you.

If you are reading this book, you can probably relate to the personal struggle that I and many of my clients have grappled with over our lifetimes. Perhaps some of these thoughts or feelings resonate with you:

- *I won't be liked if I'm powerful or outspoken.*

- *I'll be alone if I leave this person.*

- *I'm not smart enough/I'm too old/It's too late.*

- *I don't deserve it.*

- *Women can't be as successful.*

- *I'm not enough.*

- *If I were thinner, I would be able to find love.*

- *It's not safe to let my true self be seen.*

- *I'm broken/defective/incomplete.*

As a result of these thoughts and beliefs...

- Your inner critic keeps holding you back in your career. You remain quiet at work for fear of sounding too pushy or sounding stupid.

- You've achieved some success at work but still find yourself playing it safe, feel like an imposter, struggle with perfectionism, and never feel like what you do is quite good enough.

- At work you're afraid to be seen or be outspoken. You hide who you truly are and your gifts out of fear of being judged or rejected.

- In relationships you often interpret your partner's actions to mean that you're not good enough, you find yourself trying to control others' behavior, and you frequently pick relationships that reinforce beliefs that you're not worthy.

- You let promotions and opportunities pass you by and tell yourself that you're not skilled enough (despite years of experience) or that you'll look foolish.

- You hold on to toxic relationships because you don't think you deserve someone better or you're afraid of being alone.

- You are constantly criticizing yourself for who you are, what you look like or sound like.

- You think the problem is that your body isn't enough.

- You have thoughts that you are worthy and repeatedly have behaviors that sabotage these positive thoughts.

It is exactly because of all of the stories of my clients, of my own stories where I struggled with my own belief in my self-worth, that I am writing this book.

As you can see in the stories above, the people I am quoting spent many years of their lives not feeling worthy, and trying to find the answers and the avenues to find a better life and to feel better about themselves. I am hoping that this book will help to fast-track that shift in understanding of your worthiness of love, respect, safety, and belonging. Even if this struggle has been going on for you for a long time now, you can create a life with a foundation of self-worth. In that process you can allow the limiting beliefs that you have created to fall away.

If you can relate to any of the above stories, you are most likely struggling with what we call *limiting beliefs*. If you are struggling with limiting beliefs you aren't alone. They are very common, and in fact they probably happen with everyone to one extent or another. In fact, the statistics have risen to approximately 82% of people (up from 70% prepandemic) who say they've struggled with Impostor Syndrome.[1] There are many reasons that we develop these limiting beliefs and I'll be teaching you about these in this book.

First, let's look at what limiting beliefs are and what their purpose is. The definition of a "limiting belief" is **"a state of mind or belief about yourself**

---

[1] https://www.medicalnewstoday.com/articles/321730#:~:text=Ac cording%20to%20a%202020%20review,the%20experience%20ca n%20be%20lifelong

that restricts you in some way."[2] We tend to categ-orize them as negative. Please know that this is a very common phenomenon, to have limiting bel-iefs. I actually don't know anyone who has no limiting beliefs. (They may be out there!) On the following pages, you will explore your own limiting beliefs.

---

[2] https://asana.com/resources/limiting-beliefs

Chapter 2

Believe You Are Worthy

The first step in crossing over the bridge from self-doubt to self-worth is to believe: **to believe you can feel better, to believe you deserve to feel better and have a good life, to believe you *are* worthy.**

There has to be a glimmer of hope, even if you aren't sure it's possible. Something has to motivate you to move forward and to do the work it takes to get from point A to point B.

When I think of my own life, I look back and try to figure out what made me believe that more was possible. It wasn't coming from my family culture. My parents were quite religious, Irish Catholics, who seemed to follow their religion to the T. They stayed inside the lines. They were hard working middle class professionals who dedicated the majority of their adult lives to careers that helped people, nursing and nonprofit human service administration. They had seven children and seemed to be just staying afloat all the time. They made ends meet and lived within their means. This was admirable but they never seemed to dream beyond this life that was in front of them nor did they support any of us to shoot for the stars.

Of course they wanted the best for us but what that meant to them was that we should get educated, find good jobs and work to advance ourselves in a conservative manner. Their ideas of our pathways were based on their own beliefs about how to have a good life. What they believed was possible was a reflection of what they were taught and those beliefs probably contained many of their own limiting beliefs.

My parents were/are good people. They provided for us, loved us and did everything they could given who they were and what the choices were that they felt they had. Both were educated, family people. They had good values of kindness, caring for others, being social, and part of the community. They had strong religious upbringings and beliefs. They did not abuse us in any way.

When I make mention of ways where they may have missed seeing what we needed, it is because of their own upbringings where they didn't have parents who tuned in to their emotional lives. They were both products of their upbringing as we all are. I am indebted to them for bringing me into this world and teaching me all they knew about being a good person and a kind human who contributes to others with their gifts. Any time I mention shortcomings it is with all of this overarching gratitude for the bigger picture.

As a result of their upbringing and because of the tasks required by having seven children to raise, they never reflected our unique qualities back to us or spent much time focusing on us as individuals. Well, perhaps my youngest brothers felt differently but as the second to the oldest I felt like I was "one of the kids." I found my way to have approval by being "the good one" and by helping out with the younger kids. When I was school-aged, I tried to excel and got attached to a few of my teachers as a way to feel special. I was searching for the feeling of being special my entire childhood.

In my play, I would be the movie star or the "circus star" or the teacher - always one who was important and got attention. Looking back, I was searching for a better feeling about myself. This thought makes me think that there was an inherent part of me, my true self, that was always there and that was guiding me to keep searching for that feeling of joy and confidence in myself. I was searching for that feeling of being special that I now believe that we all have access to and deserve to feel.

When I was a teenager I went on a weekend religious retreat. I must have wanted to go to get away from the crowd at my house. I don't remember being particularly religious but I must have been somewhat curious. At some point during that weekend, I had somewhat of a religious awakening. I became aware of a force that took over me and elevated my feeling state to one of joy and self-love. It was a powerful experience, especially for a 16 year old. I didn't really understand it at the time, and it didn't last for very long but I think it always stayed with me. Having had that experience of feeling valuable and special was a guidepost for me of what was possible. After that time, I knew there was more to life than just what I could see. I knew I could feel more special than I did on a regular basis.

I think that my innate belief in myself and that experience was the beginning of my long journey to find that place inside again and make it more of an ongoing feeling. I did a lot of soul-searching, therapy, and personal growth research. Each step of the way I found more out about myself. Each step of the way I got closer to feeling good about who I am.

Many years later, I now know that I've been enough all along. I've been special and lovable all along. I've been worthy and deserving all along. My hope in writing this book is to give you the tools to find this self-love and acceptance also. I will be spelling out the concepts you need to know in order to see yourself more accurately with all of these qualities and to be able to live a more fulfilled life as a result.

Believe it is possible for you to feel better about yourself, to believe you are deserving of feeling worthy and of having a life that would reflect those inner beliefs. There has to be a glimmer of hope, even if you aren't sure it's possible. Something has to motivate you to move forward and to do the work it takes to get from point A to point B. We all need that motivation when we are wanting to get somewhere in life. We have insecurities and self-doubt as to whether these attitude changes are possible and doable. We wonder if we are worthy of them, or capable of them. Perhaps you have lived your life believing the opposite.

In order to get the momentum to release the old beliefs and create new ones, it takes a strong motivation and some support to make those changes. It is not always easy but it is doable. You also don't have to know how those belief changes will take place. When you start to believe it's possible (even if you don't know *how)* the steps will begin to unfold.

When I review my work with my clients and the words they have shared with me, their stories and thoughts, some of which I share in this book, I ask myself what made them take the step to work with me in hopes of feeling different. It seems that the majority of my clients find me because of someone encouraging them to try a new kind of therapy that might help them to heal. They look into the world and seem to see that some people have lives where there is more happiness and they wonder if that could be possible for them. But what is motivating them is their pain. I think that our pain is something that we should look at more as an indicator of what needs to be healed in us in order to find our self-worth. Even if your motivation is to find a way to end the pain you are experiencing, that can be what motivates you to heal and uncover your true self. That is where you naturally have self-love and belief in your worth as a precious human being.

If you are reading this book, you must believe on some level that it is possible to feel worthy. Or maybe people have been trying to tell you that you are worthy and a big part of you doesn't believe it. Perhaps there is a small voice inside that is whispering, '*Maybe I am worthy. Maybe it's possible.*'

Maybe you *want* to believe you are worthy, but there have been influences in your life that have drilled the opposite into you and hearing their voice makes you recoil from the idea.

Whatever your scenario is, if you just hold out a small portion of yourself that believes it's possible, you can move forward. Because what I know, and I think you do also, is that keeping things as they are doesn't lead to a fulfilling and rewarding life. Feeling unworthy and not enough can lead to years of emotional pain and suffering. These negative, limiting beliefs about yourself can be reflected in what we create in our lives.

The tools in this book will help you find this self-love and acceptance also.

Visualization:
Finding Your Worthy Story

Let's see if we can pinpoint your moment of recognizing that it is possible to feel worthy. Try one of the following visualizations:

1. Think about your own life experiences. See if you can remember any moments where you felt you were in the flow and experiencing life at a heightened level. Try to tap into that moment and remember what you felt like. Notice if that was a moment of experiencing your self-worth. (For that moment all of your negative judgements of yourself fell away and you were left with an experience of "knowing your worth.")

2. Remember back throughout your entire life and let your awareness settle on a time where someone made you feel worthy. Remember that moment in detail, how that person looked at you, what they said or did, how you felt inside.

3. Remember all of the movies you've seen, the books you've read or the podcasts you've listened to. Allow your attention to settle on a moment or a passage that you saw, read or heard, that rang true to you about your true worth. A moment that resonated with that inner self that is buried under the weight of all of your limiting beliefs.

This can be your story of how you came to believe in the possibility of living in your true worth. Remember this "Worthy Story" as you go through your day as a reminder of what is possible for you. There probably have been and will continue to be, many moments where you aren't feeling worthy. Take yourself back to this defining moment as a reminder of a "pep-talk" as to how you can truly feel and what your truth is.

Section II

Understand

"I always thought there was some flaw or something wrong with me causing my self-esteem to continuously be affected. Then after working on these issues (in EMDR) I experienced a sense of relief and understanding of WHY and WHERE this developed. I felt a new awareness about myself and recognized a more positive sense of self."
- Client

Chapter 3

UNDERSTAND THE LANGUAGE of BEING HUMAN

Just as we need to learn the language of our country or family in order to understand what is going on and to be able to communicate our needs and thoughts, so too is it important to understand our belief system and how it impacts our emotional world, our actions and our overall thought about who we are.

Before I learned about belief systems and personality from an EMDR perspective, I had ideas about my personality development and about how the events and people in my life shaped my feelings about myself and my persona but I wasn't clear about the whole picture. I wasn't sure what my actual personality was versus what was a defensive stance that I took. I wasn't clear about the roadmap to go about changing my perspective.

Although I read books and took courses about it, I was still confused about parts of my experience, and I'm a specialist in the field! I wasn't always sure what was driving certain beliefs I had or what I needed to do to change how I felt.

In turn, many of my therapy clients have similar experiences. They often start out telling me that they can't change something or they feel out of control in some area of their lives, and they can't understand it. They talk about feeling powerless and defeated. I've included some client experiences below.

"My sense of self-worth has improved immensely...if only because I don't have charged, negative thoughts consistently interrupting my life. Wow, what a difference."

"The first time I sought help from you I was in crisis mode. I had no clear understanding of what was causing my anger issues, and feelings of inferiority. My relationship with my wife was terrible and I knew that if I didn't try something I could enter a zone of no return in my life. After working with you, I was able to compartmentalize my emotions and properly assess the stressors in my life and minimize them. I also entered into territory that I was unprepared for and learned a lot of my emotions may have been tied to abuses from my youth."

"At its core, I was struggling with change and transition. I was laid off during Covid, and experiencing change, friends moving away, aging and stalled long-term relationships. Layer on childhood and self-confidence issues and a significant weight gain and I was in a perfect storm. I needed time and space to think through and reflect in a way that fits who I am - logical and thoughtful questions, I needed space. My journey towards healing with Suzanne was a step by step process. Exploring core issues left over from childhood and how those belief systems were influencing my life today. Facing past hurt was such an important way to get a better foundation under me and how those "hurts" influence life today. I feel stronger

today and have a greater sense of calmness, and more importantly, understand the "why" behind many of my actions today."

"My self-worth did improve as I understood the motivations of my behavior. I believe somehow I was programmed to be perfect, yet those expectations were not for good grades or to be a sports star. Little humans cannot be expected to "know" how to behave. I believe I was expected to be (like) an adult and not make mistakes. I do not blame family systems for my shame, they were doing the best they could but there is no reason to hold onto the past to define the present. I work on this everyday. I still have a journey ahead but the road is not as rocky post-therapy."

In the next section, we will go into depth about limiting beliefs. This will help you to understand yourself in a much clearer way. It's also the foundation to understand what has to shift in order to create new, empowered beliefs. When I was able to label my beliefs, track when they started, what their role was in my life, everything felt more understandable. I learned that my reactions in life, my actions were normal responses to life events. This allowed me to be more accepting of myself and it also gave me more information about how to resolve my problems. I have consistently given my clients the same message about who they are. Their personality developed as a direct result of their past experiences. Who they are makes perfect sense when they are able to understand how they developed their beliefs and behaviors.

As you have read above, my clients grow exponentially when they are able to make better sense of themselves and to see how "normal" it is to have the issues they have.

Wouldn't you like to know that you are "normal," that your emotions make sense based on where you came from? This understanding helps you to understand more clearly what might still need to get addressed.

I can't stress how powerful this awareness and reframing is. In addition to understanding yourself in a clearer manner, I'd like to suggest that you look at all of the strengths and personal qualities that you developed as you were growing up, that have brought success to you in many ways. These strengths are part of you and how you define yourself. I learned to be a caretaker which led me to become a successful therapist. That is a strength I will always have and for which I am grateful.

I point this out because when people start to do personal growth work, they often feel that they have to give up a part of who they are in order to move forward. I'd like you to see it more from the perspective that once you understand why you developed a coping pattern, you then have the option to engage in it at will rather than being controlled by it. Many of my clients who are perfectionists are afraid that if they let go of the need to be perfect (which is usually a coping skill that develops to get approval) that they will no longer take pride and have strong motivation to succeed. The idea is that the coping skill will no longer control you. Now you have choices.

Let's dive into understanding limiting beliefs: What are limiting beliefs, where do they come from and what purpose do they serve?

Chapter 4

What are Limiting Beliefs?

What are limiting beliefs and what is their impact on our lives? How do they impact our careers and our personal life? Most of the time, both of these parts of our lives become intermingled in terms of how we "show up."

In the words of Louise Hay, "If you accept a limiting belief, then it will become a truth for you." Louise Hay was a pioneer in understanding the Law of Attraction. This Law of Attraction is a belief that what you think and what you focus on is what you create. According to the Law of Attraction, the more you think about yourself in a certain way, the more it becomes your reality and you think it's your truth.

We come into this world as blank slates full of possibilities. What we learn from the environment we are raised in shapes our beliefs about who we are and what we think are our limitations, our limiting beliefs.

Limiting beliefs are "a thought or state of mind that you think is the absolute truth and stops you from doing certain things. These beliefs don't always have to be about yourself, either. They could be about how the world works, ideas, and how you interact with people."[3] Beliefs are not inherently bad,

---

[3] https://www.betterup.com/blog/what-are-limiting-beliefs

they can serve as guideposts for us and help us determine our actions in life in a good way. In fact we need to have beliefs about the world and the people in our lives. Positive beliefs help us to feel safe, to move forward and grow in our lives and to have a foundation to develop our lifestyle and values.

Beliefs are not always irrational. Beliefs can stem from actual events that happen to us and/or in the world at large. (More about this later.) Beliefs become limiting when your inner sense of who you are, and what you want for yourself is in conflict with these limiting beliefs. In the EMDR therapy world, we see that there are four core domains of beliefs.

The first core domain has to do with Safety. Positive beliefs about safety in the world are that you can be safe, you know how to stay safe, the world is safe. Negative beliefs about safety stem from experiences you might have had or witnessed. They could stem from events within your family or in society that have an impact on your beliefs about your safety in the world. Limiting beliefs about safety could be: *It's not safe to be seen, I'm not safe,* or *It's not safe to have power.* There are a whole variety of beliefs that you can have related to safety. Many of my clients were raised in families where it wasn't safe to be seen. I have heard from many clients that they hid in their bedrooms or ran out somewhere in the neighborhood when their abusive parent would come home or when there was abuse happening somewhere else in the house.

Of course, you want to have positive (and realistic) beliefs about wanting to feel that you can be safe in the world. This is a very common topic in my therapy sessions, especially with all of the events going on in the world which are making people feel unsafe. Wars, gun violence, are racial discrimination are examples of events that can be at the root of societal limiting beliefs.

A second domain of limiting beliefs has to do with your sense of value or worth. This is the most common domain of beliefs that people have trouble with. These are the limiting beliefs that people seek help to work on. *I'm not enough, I'm not smart enough, I'm not worthy, I'm not worthy of all sorts of things, I don't matter, I'm bad,* or *I'm broken.* The list goes on when it comes to worth. It could have to do with your body. It could have to do with your intellect. It could have to do with what you think you have to offer as a professional in the world.

The third core domain of beliefs has to do with your sense of control or power in your life. *I'm powerless, I'm helpless, I have no control, I can't manage.* These are some typical core negative beliefs that come in this domain.

An example from my life of negative beliefs in this domain is an experience that I had when I was in seventh grade. One day I was in science class, I was being chatty with a friend. I really don't remember what I was doing, I may have been doing something as simple as asking for a pen, but the science teacher thought it would be funny to come over to me and make an example of me. I had long hair and with his foot-long science scissors he cut a chunk of my hair, tied it in a knot and put it up on the bulletin board.

This experience created a belief in me of being powerless. It also had a component of not being safe. I felt unsafe being heard, unsafe speaking my mind as well as not safe physically as the teacher's behavior was very aggressive. (Sometimes one event alone will create lasting beliefs and sometimes the belief gets reinforced when events happen repeatedly that reinforce it.)

When events happen to us when we're younger we sometimes bury them and don't necessarily realize the impact they have on our lives until we're older. As I got older I had intense fear of public speaking. I felt unsafe with men. These turned out to be core beliefs that I had to work on resolving in order to continue growing more into my more confident self.

The fourth core domain has to do with a sense of responsibility. *It's my fault, I should have known better, I should have done something.* These are the most common negative beliefs that people express to me from this domain. When we do go back and look at their lives, there's usually things that happened where they decided subconsciously that this was a belief that they should adopt for themselves. As a young person, we may adopt a belief that we should be able to manage something but the belief is unrealistic. As children we always feel things are our fault and we feel we should've been able to do something about these events but what I help my clients see is that as children they probably had very little control over their life situations. It is very common that my adult clients have a sense of disdain for their younger selves because they have a belief that they should've been able to do something to manage an event or a toxic relationship differently. They may not even realize they have this belief until we explore it.

When I was younger, I had an experience where my father was yelling at me blaming me for pushing my sister out of the front door because he came and saw that she had fallen down the front stoop and was crying and hurt. I was standing right there at the top of the stairs in front of the door. I don't remember what happened. All I know is I believe that this event/memory had a strong lasting impact on me of feeling like it was my fault. I felt I should have done something, or I should have known better.

I remember a client who felt responsible for pushing a neighboring child down and that child got hurt. At the time, the client was probably five. At that age we aren't really capable of truly understanding what that would mean or that the situation might get out of control. I've also worked with athletes who seem to stall out when it comes to finishing their competition strong. When working with them, there is often a childhood experience where someone got hurt as a result of their empowered actions.

An example of this from my own life was when my brother rode his bike into me when I was a young child. He thought he could swerve out of the way and not hit me. He wasn't sophisticated enough to know that I might jump out of the way in the same direction that he would try to swerve away. I ended up with a big gash in my leg which led to a hospital visit and many stitches. You can imagine at the time how he might have felt. I'm sure he felt guilty and like he did a terrible thing. He probably got in trouble with my parents also. With that same sister who fell down the stairs, I had a memory of being at summer camp with her. We were partnered up as buddies, as often happened when there were activities. I decided I wanted to swim across the lake with the older kids and left her behind. When I got back I learned that while I was across the lake, my sister almost drowned. I felt guilty for years. These are the kind of events that can cause a long lasting limiting belief - *I'm bad, I should've known better, Power is bad, I can't be trusted, I should hold back.*

These situations that I just discussed are somewhat benign. Many other events in people's lives are more severe. Physical abuse and sexual abuse are events with bigger negative consequences. Most often your parents are not trying to cause you to have negative beliefs or limiting beliefs about yourself. It just kind of happens because we're human. Even when you have parents who are loving and caring, they may be stressed or anxious and yell at you and take something out on you. That is when you put the responsibility for the events on yourself. This is where your limiting beliefs may have originated but throughout your life, you maintain these limiting beliefs and they just solidify into your sense of self, of who you are. Years later, we don't make the connection between these beliefs and where and when they started.

We'll get more into this in Chapter 3, but we maintain these limiting beliefs as a way to help us cope with what's going on in our lives. When we get older we start to realize that maybe they're not helping us anymore.

What impact do these limiting beliefs have on your life? For some, this can show up as Imposter Syndrome, an umbrella term that encompasses so many variations of what looks like personality styles.

Imposter Syndrome is feeling insecure about your abilities, feeling like a fraud, afraid of being discovered as such. Most often it shows up when you are going to work and evaluating yourself, comparing yourself to other people. **Perfectionism** is the phenomenon of trying to be and look perfect in order to avoid rejection. This style develops because you don't really feel good enough about yourself. Again it has to do with insecurities. "**Playing it safe**" is another "personality type" with the purpose of avoiding rejection. All of these three personality styles are in place for people because of their limiting beliefs of not feeling safe, not feeling competent, and not feeling good enough. They may develop due to your not feeling worthy. Sometimes we develop personality traits that compensate for not having any sense of control or for feelings of powerlessness. We "play it safe." We stay on the sidelines, rather than jumping in and feeling exposed. The end result is that we avoid feeling vulnerable and we avoid imagined rejections. However these defensive coping styles can leave us feeling unheard or unseen.

Sometimes these limiting beliefs create self-fulfilling prophecies. By holding back because you don't think you're smart enough or competent enough, you also hold off on communicating your ideas. The end result is a self-fulfilling prophecy. People may not see your strengths.

I know that these self-fulfilling prophecies happened to me many times. When I was younger and working in hospital and clinic settings, I was expected to speak in meetings and at case conferences on a regular basis. I was very uncomfortable with my own competence and I didn't feel safe, so I stayed very quiet and didn't communicate unless I absolutely had to. The result was that people didn't really know what my value actually was. People didn't know what my contribution could be. I missed opportunities by not volunteering or by hesitating long enough that other people volunteered. Because people don't really know your potential, you end up not being the person chosen for projects.

What about in your personal life? As I said before, when you have limiting beliefs, however they are showing up at work, they tend to show up in a similar way in your personal life. But we don't necessarily look at it in the same way. What are some things that you might focus on when you think about yourself? You might notice you are experiencing insecurities about your appearance, your body, your cooking, your ability to take care of your children or your ability to take care of your home. You might be telling yourself you're not as good as other people. You might find that you isolate yourself from other people and don't go out with other people because you think that you're not going to be as good as them or we're insecure about our appearances. (This is definitely something I hear more from women than from men.)

Perfectionism can happen at home in your personal life also. Wanting to look perfect, to have your family look like a perfect family, to have your home look perfect, can be a way of fending off not feeling good enough which comes from a childhood experience. Your parents might have rejected you for not being perfect.

What about your love life? Unhappy relationships are a really common way that limiting beliefs get acted out. If we don't think we're worthy or deserving of love, we end up in relationships that are not happy and that are not healthy, but we don't think that we deserve any better. If we're not feeling good about ourselves, sometimes we allow ourselves to be aware of it and sometimes we don't. We think that we need to settle for toxic or unhappy relationships if we don't want to be alone. That's when we engage in avoidance strategies or numbing behaviors (alcohol, food, shopping, etc...)

One female client shared, "*When I started working with Suzanne I had been addicted to a narcissistic boyfriend for eight years and had a very turbulent relationship with him.*" This type of pattern of getting into toxic relationships is very common and difficult to break. This is also a topic that deserves an entire book of which there are many written. In this book I am just touching upon it to illustrate the impact of having a limiting belief about yourself and how it can keep you stuck in relationship patterns.

We may stay busy rather than focusing on what's going on inside of ourselves. Unfortunately these coping behaviors can often create further limiting beliefs. We aren't tuning in so our communication tends to be less direct, often causing miscommunications. This can often feed into the limiting belief of not being *good enough*, *can't do anything right*.

Sometimes we don't think that we're worthy of expressing our needs to other people. Or we think it's not okay to ask for what we need. Anxiety and depression can happen more regularly when we have a lot of limiting beliefs about ourselves, because we're really squashing that innate ability to be happy and experience joy in our lives.

In summary, when we have limiting beliefs about ourselves, it affects us everywhere we go. They start with our relationship to ourselves as individuals. Then they get acted out or played out in our interactions with others in our personal lives as well as in our careers. In the next chapter, we go into more detail about why limiting beliefs happen in our lives.

Chapter 5

Where Limiting Beliefs Come From

There are many perspectives on limiting beliefs and why we have them. I am a certified EMDR therapist. EMDR stands for Eye Movement Desensitization and Reprocessing therapy. Our perspective is that our personality is formed via hundreds and thousands of memories that come together to create a coherent sense of self. Some of these memories create limiting beliefs.

Here are **four different sources in our lives that shape our beliefs**, positive or negative. In this case, we're going to be talking about the limiting beliefs: culture, society, ancestors, and interpersonal dynamics.

Societal and Cultural Beliefs and Norms

I think that we're all familiar with **traditional societal and sometimes cultural perspectives**, tying women and men into different roles. These roles do create limiting beliefs. Here are some that come to mind. Not everyone holds these beliefs.

Women can't be powerful.

Women can't be successful.

Women should be quiet.

Women are not as good as men.

Men who show emotion are weak.

Men should be the family providers.

Both women and men are pigeon-holed in society and within different cultures into certain roles.

Many cultures have very rigid rules for the roles of women and men. Divorce, in some cultures, is considered to be a disgrace to the entire family, and the blame for the failure of the marriage goes to the woman. Women from these cultures develop all sorts of limiting beliefs about themselves whether they stay in unhappy marriages or leave.

An example, in regards to work, in the United States it has been commonly believed that to be successful at work one must give up quality time with family.

Another example of a limiting belief is that if you are a woman who is successful and competent at work, you won't be liked. This is a limiting belief but it is also statistically a reality. Women who demonstrate more direct, assertive communication and leadership styles in the workplace, tend to be less liked.

Sheryl Sandberg talks about this in her book *Lean In.*[4] According to research, women who are powerful don't tend to be liked as much at work. If you are powerful in your career it's important to keep this traditional normative belief in mind. As

---

[4] Sandberg, S. (2013.) Lean In: *Women, Work and the Will to Lead.* Deckle Edge.

our societal values change it will be more possible to be good at what you do and also be someone that people like. It's really important that we continue to work on the belief that men are more capable than women in terms of different fields, and we need to continue to challenge and question the traditional male and female roles. We need to talk about, write about and continue thinking about this topic in order to allow our society to evolve into one where people are all seen as equal.

What about money? Abundance? What kinds of limiting beliefs do you think you have or have you been taught?

I'm too old.

I'm too young.

It's selfish to want financial success.

It's too risky to try to work for myself.

We have a lot of limiting beliefs when it comes to money. Certain people and cultures look at people who have a lot of money in a negative way. In the United States there are certain careers where there may be a cultural belief that it is not right to charge a lot of money for your services. Many therapists feel that way. There is a belief that if you are helping people, you shouldn't charge them very much money. These are limiting beliefs that each person can look at and make their own decisions about. A more adaptive belief may be that *I can have a good income and have a career that is based on serving others.*

Beliefs Coming from your Ancestors

You might have limiting beliefs that were passed down from your ancestors. I'm Irish Catholic and my ancestry is one of struggle and poverty in Ireland. I inherited the belief that life is about struggle and that people can't be trusted.

Many of us come from ancestral backgrounds where there was constant conflict and war. The sense of not being able to trust that the world is safe is something that people can inherit when they are born into different families. Other versions of this are *It's not safe to be seen, We will always be oppressed,* or *In order to succeed, one must work around the clock.* I know that's one that I identify with, because of my family ancestry.

Finally, perhaps the area that I focus on the most in understanding an individuals limiting beliefs has to do with their **family dynamics or interpersonal influences.**

You might come from a family where there are neglectful parents or abusive parents in some way. You might have parents who fight with each other all the time. You might have a history of being bullied. Or you might have parents with mental or physical illness. Your parents have their own history of family dynamics and possible interpersonal events that were traumatic or dysfunctional and their trauma can get passed down to you. They may have been victims of some kind of physical sexual or emotional abuse from which they haven't healed and that can effect how they raise you. This is called intergenerational trauma.

You may also have been a victim of physical, emotional or sexual abuse. These patterns or events have an enormous impact on what you believe about yourself, in particular your self-worth. Past abuse creates a feeling of being unsafe. It affects your trust that you can be safe in the world. Your parents may directly or indirectly pass on limiting beliefs to you about these different domains of beliefs.

When you grow up within an atmosphere of abuse or traumatic events, you adopt beliefs and you hang on to them in order to survive. These beliefs become etched into your thinking patterns and create what you believe to be your personality.

Our beliefs become internalized and taken as truths. When you grow up in an atmosphere of abuse or neglect by your parents, you tend to believe that there's something negative or limiting about yourself.

The following limiting beliefs are verbalized by my clients all the time.

If I was more worthy my parents would have stopped fighting and paid more attention to me.

If I was more worthy they would have given me more positive attention and love.

If I was more worthy they would have stayed together instead of getting divorced.

If I was more worthy they would have stopped drinking or using drugs.

If I was more worthy they wouldn't have left.

If I was more beautiful they would have loved me more.

If I was thinner I would've been loved more, would have been more worthy.

As young children, we don't understand why our parents are acting the way they do. We interpret their actions from a very simple kind of "internal operating system," so to speak. We don't really understand that it's really not about us. It's really more about our parents, or the people in our lives. We don't have the experience or knowledge or processing ability to be able to step back and evaluate the situation more objectively.

Let's just say you were bullied by children in school. You might believe you are getting bullied because you're not good enough, but in reality you are getting bullied because children who bully others are not happy children. It's really more about them rather than about you, but as a child you can't discern this. If your parents were abusive in any way to you it reinforces that feeling of not being good enough when the bullying happens.

Family-of-origin dynamics lay the groundwork for all of your beliefs about yourself and they put you at risk for further situations that also reinforce your sense of self-worth.

There are other kinds of family dynamics that occur as a result of different circumstances that aren't abuse or true neglect but that are very influential in how your beliefs about yourself develop.

Some examples of these are:

- One of your siblings was sick, so your parents had to spend more time taking care of them. Since time was limited, they may have been working or taking care of your sibling, and you didn't get as much focus or attention.

- Your parents got divorced.

- Your parents were perfectionists.

- Your parents may have had body image issues.

- A parent could have gotten sick and not have been available for a period of time.

- The arrival of new babies in the family.

- You moved to a new house.

- You received medical treatments that were scary.

These events are not necessarily the result of dysfunctional interpersonal dynamics. Rather they could be more about your parents being over-whelmed with responsibilities, juggling work and family when life events happen. Sometimes you as the quiet one, the healthy one, the smart one, the totally compliant one, get lost in the shuffle or mayhem that the family as a whole is dealing with.

How does it help to know what limiting beliefs are and from where they originate? Understanding what they are and how they may have developed helps you to make sense of your life. This helps you to understand what it is that you're struggling with. It gives you a language to describe and experience your feelings and empowers you to have the choice to choose a different belief about yourself.

"I no longer believe them, so why can't I shake them?"

As adults many of my clients begin to understand and to be able to identify their limiting beliefs about themselves. They say "I know that isn't true so why can't I shake it?" Or they may say "I now see why those negative beliefs about myself developed but I no longer believe that it was because of me, so why can't I shake them?"

The answer to these questions has to do with understanding that we store feelings about ourselves and unprocessed thoughts in our bodies and until we dive back in and process them, there will be a "part of ourselves." Part of ourselves still buys into our earlier limiting beliefs. When distressing and often traumatic events occur, we may not process them immediately, so the associated feelings and beliefs may feel like they are still interfering in our lives for many years. We will go more into trauma and the impact on our bodies more in chapter six, but the important thing to know is that there is a logical reason you can't just "shake off " these beliefs and related patterns of thinking and behaviors. The power to heal comes in understanding what is going on and realizing that these beliefs are not truths, they are really just ways of coping that have been part of who you think you are for way too many years.

In review, limiting beliefs can be created by society, culture, ancestors, family, and interpersonal dynamics. Understanding where they originate from provides us the language to discuss and the power to choose new beliefs.

In the next chapter, we are going to do some personal exploration to help you identify your limiting beliefs, where they came from and how they developed.

Section III

Identify

.

"Before I felt anxious and on edge most of the time. I did not trust or value my own opinions. My self-worth was low and I put everyone else's needs and wants before my own. I always worried more about what everyone else thought or felt. Some traumas were and are so deep I didn't recognize them as reasons for the behaviors I had. After working with (Suzanne) I have learned that self-care is a priority. Because I was able to process past incidents and memories, traumas. I have learned to value myself and trust my own feelings, instincts about people and places and things as well as situations." - Client

Chapter Six

Trauma & Limiting Beliefs

Learning about and understanding trauma can be therapeutic because it sheds a completely different light on your behavior, your feelings and your thoughts. Once you understand what trauma is and how it impacts people, you have more choices for how to understand yourself and make better choices for yourself. In this section you will be learning more about trauma and you will have the opportunity to identify your limiting beliefs and track them to their origins.

Remember the entire point of this book is to help you reclaim your sense of self-worth. Trauma is something that takes that sense of self-worth away. You can work on getting it back.

Let's look at what trauma is, how it influences our limiting beliefs, and how it impacts our feelings of self-worth. In my experience, having limiting beliefs is very often a result of traumas. There are different ideas about what constitutes trauma. In the field of psychotherapy and trauma treatment, we differentiate between what we call "big T" and "little T" traumas.

Trauma is the reaction to a very disturbing event. There are different kinds of life events that cause enough distress to create trauma. "Big T" trauma is probably what you think of when you think about trauma: major accidents that happen, car accidents, airplane accidents, or any other kinds of unusual accidents where somebody is injured or passes away as a result, physical abuse, sexual abuse, natural disasters, such as hurricanes, tornadoes, and floods. These are all events where people may die, may witness others dying and/or experience devastation. The COVID-19 pandemic is classified as a global trauma. With trauma, there is a fear of losing your life, usually, and this experience totally overloads your brain's ability to cope.

Then we have what we call "little T" trauma. Most people experience this level of trauma without even realizing the impact that it has on us. "Little T" trauma could be your parents getting divorced, your parents fighting a lot, your parents being withholding of attention or outward expression of love toward you for various reasons including their own discomfort with showing affection, parents who are perfectionists and you feel you never please them, moving to a new neighborhood when you're growing up, moving to a new school, losing friends losing a pet, or a sibling being sick. In the case of the sick sibling that means that the parent has to focus their attention on your sibling leaving you with less attention. Other examples are being bullied or having a teacher who makes mean comments to you. I had a teacher compare me to a "whore" when I was in 8th grade because I had on a miniskirt (along with every other girl in the class) and it had a negative impact on how I felt about myself. I felt vulnerable, like I was "bad." His comment to me made me feel exposed and unsafe.

You could have trauma from having a parent who had mental illness. They may have been present but not emotionally attuned to you so you feel neglected or ignored. This can make you feel not important or unlovable. Another example is when parents have alcoholism, which could go into the "big T" or the "little T" trauma, depending on how serious it is. Parents who are verbally abusive cause trauma. You don't necessarily even realize it when you're growing up, but it's traumatic because it makes you feel like you don't deserve to be treated with love and respect.

When you're growing up, you don't always realize that how your parent is treating you is wrong because you don't have anything to compare their behavior to. However, as you get older and you move out into the world and compare yourself with other people and other families, you start to realize that how you were treated wasn't right. Many of my clients say that they never considered the events in their lives to be causing trauma, or that they experienced trauma in their lives. When we discuss the definition of trauma and break it down to the events in their lives, they see it more clearly. This is often a very powerful realization and brings on healing.

I was working with a professional woman who had lost a lot due to alcoholism. When we reviewed her life, it was clear to me that she had experienced relational trauma. She had no idea it was categorized as trauma. She says, *"I was connected with Suzanne during an in-home treatment for alcoholism. During this time I suffered from extreme anxiety. I spent over two years with Suzanne in counseling...The thought of trauma had never occurred to me, though it made sense as she counseled. There was a big shift in understanding of the root of my anxiety."*

Another professional woman I was working with came to work with me for help with her fear of driving on the highway. Through our work she began to understand that she had experienced many traumas. *"I was working as a therapist and was experiencing panic episodes when I drove on the highway. Little did I know that it was not about driving. Through EMDR I was able to ascertain that I had experienced at least 20 significant traumatic events in my 60 years."*

All of these traumas create limiting beliefs about ourselves, or about the world. You might believe the world is not safe or you're not safe. You may not feel good enough. You may not believe that you deserve love and respect. You may not feel that it's safe to voice your opinions and your thoughts. Another woman I worked with spent years believing she was the cause of traumas that happened to her. *"I was stuck in old trauma, unable to build healthy relationships. I blamed myself for things I had no control over in my childhood."* If you had an irritable parent who would get angry at you, when you were talking about whatever you talked about, that is trauma. It's trauma because you are experiencing rejection from the person you depend on the most in your life.

Let's look at what happens in your body when you experience trauma.

When you experience trauma, your brain shuts down. It gets overloaded. Your prefrontal cortex goes "off-line" and you react from your more primitive brain. It's so upsetting that you're not able to process what happens to you or what's happening to you so it gets stored in your brain, but it doesn't get processed. It's like having a file in a computer that doesn't have a name on it. It continues to affect you randomly in ways that cause interference in how you feel about yourself or how you feel in your life. You can also develop symptoms in your body that represent unprocessed trauma.

Here is what some of my clients report before they resolved their traumas:

"I would feel an ache in my chest and a pit in my stomach."

"I was depressed with crippling anxiety. I have severe food sensitivities, was diagnosed with TMJ when I was nine years old, had incapacitating environmental allergies, had excruciating back pain and felt lost in my life. Unbeknownst to me I also had suppressed grief and traumatic memories from early childhood that were buried so deep in my brain, but that were informing every single reaction I had to the world around me."

"I was experiencing completely debilitating anxiety and panic attacks that would seemingly come out of nowhere. I had lingering self-doubt and feelings of unworthiness that would creep in trying to sabotage my personal and professional business relationships."

"There were unresolved traumas of all different types and major body issues."

"I was an emotional mess...I cried suddenly and often. I had fears of loss, afraid of the future, panic attacks."

"Outwardly I gave the impression of being confident, at peace in my own skin. I was actually living a double life! Inside I experienced debilitating feelings of unworthiness, endless ruminating over how my actions or inaction affected others. Alone in my bed at night, I would lay awake fearful of sleep because of the nightmares that plagued me from childhood."

Trauma and the Brain

Probably all parts of your brain are affected when you experience trauma. The amygdala, hippocampus, or prefrontal cortex are all impaired.

What happens when we have trauma is that we go into fight or flight. The amygdala, which is the part of our brain that kicks up and creates that fight or flight response in order to try to survive the experience. What happens is the experience doesn't get processed and the brain stays in that fight or flight state. The result of that perpetual fight or flight state is that people who have had trauma tend to have a lot of anxiety. As a trauma survivor, your brain is revved up all the time looking for the next shoe to drop or the next bad thing to happen.

Another part of your brain that is affected by trauma is the hippocampus. The hippocampus is the part of the brain that processes memories, stores them and also helps us know when we're safe and when things are okay. With repeated trauma, that part of the brain shrinks and it doesn't function as well. One consequence of this is that as an adult when you think about your past traumas, your memory is not so clear, it's a little foggy.

The third part of the brain that is affected by trauma is your prefrontal cortex. The prefrontal cortex is what helps you to solve problems, make sense of things, looks at situations in a rational way. When you have trauma, what we say is that your prefrontal cortex goes offline. You are no longer thinking, you're just reacting and you're in fight or flight mode.

Most of my clients get to a point in their work where they come up against confusion or judgment toward themselves for not behaving differently than they wish they had when they look back on their trauma. Remember, after the fact, when you are looking back at your past traumas, you may have emotional distress but you are not in a traumatic situation. You are thinking more clearly. It's a very different experience than when the trauma was actually happening. There can be a sense of relief when you understand the dynamics that happen when you have trauma. Logic is out, reflexive action is in charge. Subconsciously your body decides what the best course of action is for survival.

All of these brain reactions create the perfect storm and stop you from being able to function in your best and highest manner. As the years go by we don't know to connect the dots between past traumas and our current behavior. We think that how we are reacting to our work situations, our relationships or our feelings about ourselves, are normal reactions. We just think it's who we are. In reality we may still be reacting to past trauma that is being triggered in many ways. Past traumas create limiting beliefs and because of these beliefs, we don't necessarily react in the healthiest and highest manner possible.

Learning about trauma shines light onto many situations. You can start to say, "Oh, wow, I think I feel this way because of trauma that happened to me when I was growing up. I felt like I wasn't worthy or important and now I interpret many interactions as worse than they are."

Now when you go into the office, and people don't necessarily greet you in the way that you want them to, it triggers that feeling of not being worthy. It triggers the memory of being neglected. If other people get more attention at work, it could trigger that old memory of not getting attention and that brings up those negative beliefs about yourself.

When we have trauma in our past and it's not healed, it is absolutely going to have an impact on your here-and-now feelings about yourself. You will struggle with feeling worthy, feeling whole, feeling lovable. You might have body image problems, or any other kind of a problem that you focus on about yourself where you don't feel good enough, and you aren't able to feel positive feelings about yourself. Those are your limiting beliefs. Those beliefs can be because of "big T" or "little T" trauma.

Breaking the Cycle

The most important thing here is to be able to look at what we're doing in everyday life and what our limiting beliefs are that come up. Understanding what limiting beliefs are and why we have them allows us to connect the current negative belief to a past experience of trauma, perhaps when you were a child.

Maybe you were bullied by kids. If you understand trauma and how it impacted you, as an adult you can see how that experience made you believe you weren't good enough. It might have made you believe that you weren't going to be safe when you showed up in the world or made yourself known. Maybe you said certain things when you were young and that triggered kids to bully you. I had a client who realized he had been very insecure as a young adolescent and he had overcompensated and said things he wished he hadn't. Like many people, if we feel not good enough, it gets played out in many ways and can then create more situations to occur that might reinforce the limiting belief we already had about ourselves.

Another example of this is when you are in work situations or social situations, you may have fear about just being yourself and saying what you think. You may have difficulty trusting that people will respond to you in a healthy and respectful way. Instead, you expect something bad to happen. We may have this limiting belief of not being heard or not being good enough. Then we create a situation where we're not heard because we aren't being vocal. It's a vicious cycle, but to understand that all this is happening helps you to break that cycle at different places and to be able to look at things in a different way.

Understanding trauma allows you to use your coping skills more effectively so that you end up continuing to feel more confident and feeling better.

When you understand your trauma triggers better, you are more able to stop, take a moment, breathe and observe when things happen in your life. You are able to identify the limiting beliefs that get triggered. You have the space to ask yourself what is happening here? Why do I have this limiting belief right now? It doesn't make sense. Where did I start to feel this way? How long have I been feeling this way?

Understanding trauma allows you to have a blueprint for understanding your limiting beliefs and why they're there. It helps you to see that your reactions are normal reactions that you had when you were younger or at an earlier time in your life. As an adult you also know that your limiting beliefs and reactions are not necessarily realistic in your current situations. You have options to make different choices and to use more logical communication. You can adapt healthier beliefs about yourself. You can decide to come from a place of self-worth.

Putting Together the Puzzle Pieces

Before moving on to the next section, this might be a good time to go to your journal to process any of your thoughts related to this section about trauma. Did you maybe have some traumas in your life that you were not really aware of or that you did not look at as trauma? This is like putting pieces of a puzzle together and to see the picture of your life more clearly. Take some time to look at your life as a continuum of events that occurred and beliefs about yourself that were created. Notice any patterns of these beliefs getting repeated throughout your life.

Notice patterns of interactions and reactions you have in the here and now that might be trauma reactions that are triggered. The whole picture should make better sense.

It can be difficult to think about these experiences, so I encourage you to use self-compassion and get support whenever needed.

Chapter Seven

Where Do Your Limiting Beliefs Come From?

You've read about limiting beliefs; where they come from, the domains, and how they can be created. You've read about trauma; what trauma is, the different categories and how it affects you on different levels. Now it's important for you to gain some clarity on your own limiting beliefs.

Keep in mind that reading this book is not a replacement for therapy. If you are feeling very fragile or having a lot of emotional turmoil right now that is causing you difficulty in your everyday life, you may want to postpone doing the exercises until you are feeling more steady. You also may want to read this book and practice this exploratory exercise in conjunction with seeing a psychotherapist for additional support. In the resources section of this book, I have a link to the EMDR International Association. On that website you will find a directory of EMDR therapists in your state who may be able to work with you.

In this chapter you will find an exercise that will help you track your own limiting beliefs and be able to identify when they were created.

One of the most common things I find with my clients is that they don't realize how their current issues are connected to their earlier lives. It makes perfect sense that there is confusion as we haven't been taught emotional intelligence and personality development. Of course there tends to be confusion and disbelief.

The other common phenomenon is a sense of shame that people report that they are still grappling with issues and events that occurred many years ago in their lives. They feel there is something wrong with them for being in this place. In all my years as a therapist, it has become very clear to me that we all have past issues that have been left behind but continue to affect us in our lives. The good news is that we can heal from those past issues and move forward.

As an EMDR therapist, I was trained to facilitate the exploration of current issues and where they originated using different techniques. One of these is the Float Back exercise, which is a standard EMDR technique designed by Francine Shapiro, the founder of EMDR therapy.[5] Below you will find my version of the Float Back exercise, where we focus on one area of difficulty in your life. This exercise can be used to look at all the areas in your life that may be causing you distress.

---

[5] Shapiro, F. (2012). *Getting past your past : take control of your life with self-help techniques from emdr therapy*. Rodale Books.

Float Back Exercise

It's time to clear your head and focus on you. In the next page, I'm going to lead you through a short exercise called the Float Back to help you explore and identify what your most common limiting beliefs are and where they may have come from. To get ready, get comfortable and find a quiet space where you are alone and feel safe to close your eyes and go within yourself. You can sit or lie down. Have a journal at hand so that you can capture your experience and any insights you have. there by responding to the reflection questions. Sit back, close your eyes, put all the other things that you've been thinking about in your day-to-day life right now, over to the side and start to focus on your breath. Breathe in and breathe out and just notice your breath. Breathing in and breathing out. Just settle into that for a minute.

Now I'd like you to think about a situation that's going on in your life that is causing you distress. It may be related to your work, your personal life, your relationship, or your thoughts about yourself or your body.

Picture that situation in your mind. Just kind of see it happening. As you do that, I want you to pay attention to what those negative thoughts about yourself are that come up in your mind about yourself when you think about being involved in that situation.

Sometimes the negative/self-limiting belief isn't readily clear to you. Try to notice the thoughts that feel as close to a negative thought or limiting belief.

Keeping those negative thoughts/beliefs in mind, I want you to just imagine floating back in time. Continuing to go back through time until the first time that you remember having those thoughts about your-self; until the first time in your life that you recall those negative/self-limiting beliefs/feelings present in your life.

When you think about this situation, and the thoughts about yourself, and when you pinpoint a situation, just notice, how old are you? What's the situation that's coming up? What is the situation you are remembering that is associated with those negative thoughts?

Did it have to do with family? Did it have to do with friends, schools, society, culture, more than one situation? Notice what kinds of thoughts come to you when you try to pinpoint it. See yourself in those situations, notice the dynamics that occurred and notice from your adult self's vantage, why you might have adopted the negative/self-limiting beliefs that you did. (I will come back to this later to talk more about how our limiting beliefs serve us.)

Once you are able to do that I want you to kind of slowly travel forward in your life. Notice where that belief about yourself got reinforced.

What are the situations in your life that you got involved in? By choice or just by course of action like school or work? Were the events distressful? Do you remember that these events could have reinforced those earlier negative/self-limiting beliefs?

(Chances are, the events you are remembering caused a great deal of distress when they occurred. If they're really really hard to get rid of now, chances are they've been reinforced several times throughout your life.)

Continue to notice the events and related negative beliefs that are attached to them until you arrive back in the here now and you see yourself in the current situation giving you so much trouble you had identified.

When you are finished with that process, take a nice, slow, deep breath, let it go. Open your eyes, come back to the room wherever you're sitting or laying.

I recommend that you now go to your journal and start to write about what you realized when you did this exercise. Remember all you learned in the previous chapters also about limiting beliefs. What did this visualization help you realize about yourself, about your life, about where your current negative/self-limiting beliefs actually came from?

What are your thoughts about it? Whatever comes to you, just start to journal. In doing this exercise you may become more aware of how these limiting beliefs continue to pop up. You may see patterns where those kinds of situations and beliefs might still be being reinforced in different ways today.

Repeat this exercise as often as you want with different current situations in mind. Notice the limiting belief and do the Float Back again to see what the strand of events are that are reinforcing your current beliefs. If you do this enough you start to feel freedom from your current stressors.

What my clients often become aware of and what I believe, is that situations continue to occur in our lives until we heal from the limiting beliefs that accompany them.

This is so helpful to realize because for one, it gives you your power back. You can realize that it is your issue that is most important and if you can heal from it you can create and attract healthier experiences. Once we heal from the inside out, we then create an external world that will now reinforce our glowing inner world!

Take some time weekly to reflect on the limiting beliefs that have become automatic for you. I invite you to practice noticing every time these "frequent flyers" come up and note it in your journal.

Some other things to notice could be:

- Which type of belief tends to pop up for you most often?

- Are there particular people, environments, or situations that seem to trigger these beliefs for you?

- Are there times when you seem to be operating with your newer, healthier beliefs and "operating system." What are those situations?

- Who, what, when and where are the situations when you seem to feel the best ?

This completes our discussion about trauma, and where your limiting beliefs come from. In the next section, I am going to give you some tools to help you to understand, cope with and resolve these limiting beliefs. Feel free to review these first two sections anytime you feel you need clarification.

Section IV

Learn

"I know that I am worthy of compassion and respect and love and so much more. Now the work that remains is to put this into practice in every aspect of my life." - Client

Chapter Eight

Visualization Tools for Coping with Difficult Emotions

Coping tools are really important. To understand what is happening in our lives, we keep using the same explanation in our head. We use the same explanation that we've been using over and over again, even if we've been told that there are other explanations that could be happening, or that could be used to understand something that's happening. We continue to use our old ones because that is the well-worn neural pathway that we have been finessing our entire lives.

An example is, if somebody says, "Hey, you look great today." If all the time you've been telling yourself, *I look like crap, I never look good, Nobody's ever going to think I'm attractive,* the new information won't register. That may be the story you've been telling yourself for many, many years. That is the neural pathway that we're going to slide right back into, even if somebody's told us, otherwise. People may tell you did a great job, but on the inside, you're saying *Oh, yeah, right. If they really knew,* or *They're just saying that* or whatever your explanation in your head is. Without learning these new coping tools, without creating some new neural pathways, it's really hard to make a shift. That's why if you've been trying your whole life to make changes by reading books, or taking courses or going to talk therapy, then it might help some, but it doesn't help completely because you're not really getting deep enough into those neural pathways that are so strong.

In order to begin to process our world in a healthier way that will lead to a better outcome, we need to learn new ways of processing and coping. This section will teach you more about this perspective and will teach you some tools that you can use to begin to create a new reality in your life.

In this chapter, I'm going to lead you through some different exercises that are going to create internal resources. Internal resources are skills that we have on the inside. We use them with how we think about situations, how we react to situations. Creating new internal resources is going to generate new neural pathways. In doing so, because these pathways are created already, we tend to use them when events occur in our lives. If they are positive and strength connected, they help us to naturally have a more adaptive manner of understanding and coping.

When athletes are in training for a competition they visualize their entire meet from start to finish. They see themselves being successful. They've already created a neural pathway to succeed. Consequently, when they are actually competing in the meet, they slip into their event much easier, and it feels like it makes sense to them. Their bodies seem to remember the competition.

This is what we're doing. We're trying to shift all those internal pathways so that they allow you to access a more empowering and positive image about yourself, who you are and what your life looks like.

These are visualizations used by many different types of therapists and have been found to be very effective. I particularly learned to use them in my training as an EMDR therapist. They are commonly used when working in a certain phase of EMDR therapy. The Support Circle comes from my adaptation from Laurel Parnell "tapping in" work. Her book *Tapping In* offers many more very useful visualizations.[6] I have utilized them over the years and have adapted them in different ways.

Next we'll go through three different visualizations that you can do that will give you tools to use anytime in your life when you need them. In particular, these tools can be used when you are feeling emotional distress.

Three Visualizations

These visualizations help to create new ways of experiencing the things that are going on with you whether it's difficult emotions, negative self talk or limiting beliefs that are coming up during situations and where you're not able to really think clearly.

Using these tools will help you to get your clear-minded thinking back on track. You can always go back and look at the negative stuff that was coming up another time.

------

[6] Parnell, L. (2008) *Tapping In: A Step by Step Guide To Activating Your Healing Resources Through Bilateral Stimulation.* Sounds True.

Visualization 1

Safe Calm Place Visualization

As we start this visualization, take a moment to get into a comfortable position. Perhaps you want to make sure you have no distractions for a few minutes. You may want to have your journal by your side to do some journaling when you complete the visualization.

Perhaps close your eyes, and what I'd like you to do is to think about going somewhere in the world where you would feel very calm and peaceful and happy. Now, this could be a real or imaginary place, somewhere you have been before, or just someplace that you've never been, but you think that you'd like to go there.

In general, it's best to imagine yourself there by yourself, not with other people in your life. If that doesn't work for you, go ahead and just do this in the way that feels good to you. If the only way you can imagine being in this calm place is with a trusted person, then that's ok. The whole idea is to help yourself feel calm and peaceful. Do it to the best of your abilities.

With your eyes closed imagine that you are in that place that you've already determined you want to go. There can be more than one place that you use, but for this time, let's just choose the one that feels the best for you today.

As you imagine yourself there I want you to use your senses to imagine that you're actually there. Your body and your brain don't know the difference between what you're imagining, and what's actually happening.

Picture the scene where you are. What are the colors? What does the environment look like? Is it out in nature somewhere? A beach, a mountain, by a river? It can be anywhere you want it to be. Notice.

What time of year does it feel like? Does it feel like summer, fall, winter, or spring? What is the temperature? Is it hot and sunny? Is it cold? Is it snowing? Wherever it is, really see it around you as if you're there. Notice.

What are the sounds that you might hear? What are the colors that you might be seeing and the body sensations. Are you walking on hot sand or standing or sitting somewhere with your feet in hot sand or are you floating in refreshing water? What is the body sensation that you're feeling? How does your body feel right now as you are imagining being there? Notice.

Notice if you're by yourself there, if there are other people around? Are there any animals in your calm place? Without controlling it, let your mind create this picture that only you can see.

Now what I'd like you to do is to give this place a name. In your mind just give it a one word or two word name or phrase. When you think about that name, this is the place that you're going to come back to whenever you think about it and I want you to repeat that name a couple times while you are still in this visualization. Notice where you might feel the calmness in your body when you imagine yourself there and when you speak that name of your safe calm place. Where does your body feel peaceful and calm?

When you're done, you can take a nice deep breath. Let it out and then come back to the room.

The more you practice this, the stronger the feeling of calm will get. Also, when you think of the name of your calm place, you will be able to get to that calm state faster.

Some things can happen when you are creating your calm, safe place. Sometimes it takes practice getting yourself to be able to get to a place like this. Sometimes, we need to do a little more research on being able to create it in our mind. Maybe find a picture of a place that you think is amazing that you might want to imagine going to. Or watch videos or reels of places that look interesting and appealing to your idea of what might feel like a relaxing/calming place to be.

You might have also had a hard time while you were there (wherever you were imagining that you were).

You might notice that things happen or thoughts come up where you start to feel anxious or stressed. What you can do when that happens is say okay, I'm in charge here. What do I need to add to this picture so that it feels safer, calmer, more protected from any intrusions of thoughts or imagine a protective person coming into the picture.

You may find it's difficult to stay in one place. Your mind may hop around to different locations. Sometimes my clients who have a lot of anxiety say their minds won't settle down. When this happens I just tell them to create a story in their mind that takes them to different locations, kind of like going on a trip and moving to different locations everyday. Or maybe they want to make their place more of an activity where they are moving around, like playing a sport. I have them use all of their senses and fill in the picture with all of the details.

Whatever you create that helps you get into a calm, safe and peaceful state is ok. Nobody is judging you. There is no right or wrong.

Finally, if you find that you keep incorporating someone into your calm/safe place who doesn't help you feel calm and safe, I suggest that you gently try to allow yourself some distance from this person. If this isn't possible for you to do for any reason, you might want to try the next visualization and come back to this visualization at a later date.

In order for this calm/safe place visualization to be most effective, it requires practice. I recommend that you practice this visualization daily, perhaps at a certain time of day when you are taking time for yourself or meditating, when you are in a calm state. In doing this you will create some fresh neural pathways that go along with it. Then when you are going about your day, practice using this at times when you might be mildly upset about something.

Finally, this is a tool to use when you are feeling distressed about anything, as a way to shift yourself into a calmer state of mind. In doing this, you can bring yourself out of a fight or flight state and into a calmer state when you will have greater access to your problem solving ability.

If you use the name of it at the same time when doing the visualization, what happens eventually is that if you say the name of this place, like "secret getaway," or "Grand Canyon with the kids" (that was mine), the name and the "calm state" become linked. The neural pathway becomes deeper and you get to that calm state quicker. Practice, practice, practice.

Visualization 2

Container Visualization

The next visualization that we're going to do is called the Container Visualization. In this visualization, you are going to create a container in your mind. It has three criteria: 1) it has to be strong, 2) it has to have a top and 3) it has to have some kind of a mechanism for locking. Find a comfortable spot to sit and do this visualization, with no distractions. Keep your journal close to jot down your thoughts after you finish the exercise.

Close your eyes and imagine a very strong container. Everybody's container looks different. You can make your container look however you want it to look. (Big, small, square, round, etc.) What is yours made of? What is the texture on the outside? How big is it? How heavy is it? What color is it? Does it say anything on the outside? How do you lock it?

You can reinforce this by taking a piece of paper and drawing your container and stick that in with your journal. The more ways that you can reinforce this container, the stronger it will be.

What we're going to do with this container is call upon this container whenever you have thoughts that don't feel good, or memories that are upsetting or emotions that are distressing you and interfere with your ability to focus on something that you're trying to do. When you notice this happening, you're going to imagine putting those thoughts, feelings, events, people, into this container that you have created, and you're going to be shutting the top, locking it and just pushing it away. Remember that your brain thinks this is an actual container with actual results that happen.

Then what I'd like you to do is to practice thinking about a situation where you start to feel a little bit distressed, not a 10 on a scale of 1 to 10 but something that might be more of a 2. Now think about that situation.

What is the distressing element? Is it thoughts, feelings? Does your body start to feel tension somewhere? Is it a person that's stressing you out? Memories that are coming up? Now I want you to imagine putting them in the container, shutting it, locking it and then pushing it away. Then take a nice deep breath and notice how it feels once those feelings, memories and/or thoughts are contained.

You can come back to them anytime you want. They're not gone. This is a way of creating internal body boundaries and compartmentalization in your brain.

Creating these internal boundaries with visualizations is something that might come easy to some people and may be more challenging to others. Remember to practice all of these exercises with compassion and gentleness towards yourself!

My experience is that when you have a lot of limiting beliefs, it's harder to compartmentalize and so this is a really important visualization and exercise to do as often as it takes to feel like you have mastered it. Don't give up. It might take a while to get to the point where it feels like it's working.

Take a moment now and do some journaling about this. On a daily basis, practice it by using little things that happen, such as minor annoyances and irritations. Notice how it feels when you see yourself having control over your feelings and thoughts. In my experience, it's going to start to feel really good. It helps you feel empowered to be able to make choices and have an impact on your state of mind.

We do not need to be at the mercy of our emotions and feelings!

Our third visualization is called the Support Circle Visualization. It is a very, very powerful visualization, because we're acknowledging people in our lives. Very often when my clients complete this visualization, they are overwhelmed with how loved they feel and how connected they feel to at least a couple of people who have been very important people to them. This is also powerful because it helps people shift to a realization of the good that is in their lives rather than always focusing on the negative.

There are people who are here now or people who have been part of our lives in the past, who have had an enormous positive impact on our lives. Even if there's somebody who's no longer part of your life, if they've had a positive impact on your life, you can draw upon the energy of those experiences that you've had with them.

In this visualization we connect with the strength of those relationships. This is all about the energy of relationships in our lives. It reinforces the feelings of those relationships being there for us at all times. We just have to call upon it. It will be there for us. The images and feelings that go along with that energy are what we call internal resources. Because these are actual people with whom you have inter-acted with already, you are lighting up the connect-ed neural pathways. By grouping several positive people into one visualization we are creating a "superhighway" because we are linking several neural pathways!

Visualization 3

Support Circle Visualization

Find a quiet spot to sit and concentrate on this visualization, where you won't be distracted. Keep your journal nearby so you can jot down your thoughts after you are finished.

Think of three or four people who have been very significant in your life, people who have made you feel loved and supported, cared for and worthy. You can jot down their names if you want. You can start out with one or two people if that's all you can think of. Sometimes it's your pets. Whoever you add to this support circle today, you can always add more people to it as you go.

I want you to, again, close your eyes. Take a deep breath, let it go. I want you to think about one of those people and imagine that they're standing right in front of you right now. I would like you to imagine what it is that they would say and do to let you know they love you and see them saying it and doing it.

Hear them, see them, feel it. What is their way of showing you that they care about you and they support you? They believe in you. They know that you have what it takes. See how they say that and how they show you that. Hear it happening in your mind. Notice how it feels.

Take a deep breath. Let it go.

Now I want you to imagine just turning slightly and seeing another one of those people in front of you. I would like you to imagine what it is that they would say and do to let you know they love you and see them saying it and doing it.

Hear them, see them, feel it. What is their way of showing you that they care about you and they support you. They believe in you. They know that you have what it takes. See how they say that and how they show you that. Hear it happening in your mind. Notice how it feels.

Again, take a deep breath, let it go when you're done and turn again and see that third person there.

I would like you to imagine what it is that they would say and do to let you know they love and support you and see them saying it and doing it.

Hear them, see them, feel it. What is their way of showing you that they care about you and they support you. They believe in you. They know that you have what it takes. See how they say that and how they show you that. Hear it happening in your mind. Notice how it feels.

It's different for every person in our lives. When you're ready, take a deep breath and let it go.

Now I want you to imagine those people standing around you in a circle and maybe reaching out and each one placing their hand on your shoulder in a different place and imagine just knowing that they're all there with you. Feel their energy, feel their love. Feel that support from that circle and know in your mind that they are always there for you.

Notice how this feels in your body. Where do you feel this support and love when you think about it in your body? Try to lock it into a location. Whenever you want to think of this Support Circle imagine it in that location of your body.

Now take a deep breath and let it go. Come back to the room. Take a moment to journal about your experience: how it felt, who is in your circle, what you realized, any other thoughts that come up.

This is YOUR support circle and you can add more people to this circle anytime you want.

Practice having this group of people with you in your day-to-day life when you go about your business whether you're at work, whether you're at home, have a dialogue with them. Keep that internal dialogue going.

These are people who are like your cheerleaders. These people have your back. They're in your corner. If you're struggling with feeling confident at work, let's say you have to speak in public a lot or you have to interact with a team of people with whom you feel very intimidated, keep this circle with you and imagine they're there.

If you hear yourself talking negatively or having self-doubt or if criticisms are coming up in your mind, imagine what your support circle would be saying to you right now. Imagine what they would say or show you to stop doing that. How would they support you to know that *you can do this* or *you've got what it takes.*

You can draw upon this support circle anytime. You can call upon just one person at times and/or you can have all of them. It's your decision.

Now you have these three tools that you can draw upon anytime you want. The more you practice them, the stronger they will be.

Next, we'll look at using cognitive strategies to manage self-limiting beliefs.

Chapter Nine

Cognitive Tools to Resolve Limiting Beliefs

In this chapter, you will learn cognitive strategies that are going to help you to cope with difficult emotions so that you don't get "hijacked."

The word cognitive is related to the word cognition which has to do with "conscious intellectual activity" according to the Webster dictionary. Strategies are "plans of action" that you use by thinking about things in a different way. Because how you interpret what's happening in your life is a very big percentage of what shapes our behavior, having cognitive strategies come in handy!

Cognitive strategies help you to get through some tricky situations without getting hijacked with a lot of emotions. When you do get hijacked, or triggered, you go into "fight or flight" and when that happens, your prefrontal cortex goes "offline," and you're no longer able to think clearly.

When I was in my twenties and living in a sketchier part of New York City, I got held up by two men, probably looking for some drug money. I immediately began fighting back and trying to prevent them from taking my purse. After one of them punched me, I think I snapped back to my senses and realized I should just let go of the bag and slump down. They took my bag and ran away. I got out of there very quickly after that. In that example, I moved into fight or flight without even thinking. It was a reaction. After a few minutes, I saw what I was doing and started to have access to my thought process again and quickly evaluated the situation to take action with the safest plan I could think of. What we're trying to do is to prevent that from happening in our lives. We are trying to arm ourselves with strategies to use to be able to manage difficult emotions and to not get hijacked with fear and move into a reactive state.

After I got mugged in New York City the first time, I learned some strategies to use in the event that it ever happened again. Well, as it turned out, it *did* happen again, but the second time I was armed with strategies and I was able to maintain my ability to think clearly and used the strategies to minimize any disruption for me.

Think about your own life. How often have you looked back on a situation and asked yourself why you reacted the way you did?

Let's get started with a few strategies. We can talk more about trauma in the next chapter to further understand those triggered reactions, or trauma reactions.

Cognitive Strategy #1
What is Reframing and What Does it Allow?

The first cognitive strategy that I want to share is reframing how you are looking at what is happening in your life. This is a strategy that comes from a Cognitive Behavioral Therapy (CBT) framework. In this case, we are reframing our self-talk. If I'm in a staff meeting, and I'm talking and people are looking at me and not saying anything, I might habitually think, *Oh, my God. They think that I'm a fool. They think I'm not very smart or I don't know what I'm talking about.* That is my limiting belief that's coming up. The minute I start to hear myself thinking those things and talking in that way to myself (because we do talk to ourselves), you see that you are interpreting a situation that way, reframe it.

My clients sometimes question this. They wonder how they can reframe it if they don't have the proof of what might be really going through other people's minds. I tell them that even if the reframe isn't true, they can find a way to reframe what's happening. You could say to yourself, *Wow, these guys are speechless. They really don't even understand what I'm talking about,* or *They think this is so amazing. Maybe they're insecure because of what I'm saying that they didn't come up with these thoughts themselves.*

In your personal life, an example of this could be in the realm of dating. If somebody you're dating doesn't want to go out with you again, rather than thinking, *I knew it, I knew that no one's going to want me because I'm not good enough in different ways.* Reframe that. *Wow. You know, first of all, this person, if they don't like me, it's probably a good sign that they're not the right person for me. They don't see how special I am. Its probably good that they're not pursuing me.* That's one way to reframe it. Or *Maybe it's just not the right time for them. They don't have the energy/freedom right now, to get into a relationship.* Those are two possible ways to reframe that.

Sometimes we can use this strategy to tame our own inner critic. It's not always about what other people are saying or doing. Sometimes it's more about yourself. Let's just say you have to do a presentation. You are your worst critic. You're talking to yourself in a really derogatory way about what it is you're putting together. If you notice this, reframe your thoughts. You could say, *You know what, you always think the worst of yourself. That is not necessarily the best way to go about this. I'm going to start to think in a more positive way and I betcha what I'm doing is going to be good enough.* It's just reframing the self-talk that you're hearing. I tell people when they're driving, if somebody cuts them off, rather than getting really angry at them, reframe it, turn it around somehow and say *That person must be having an emergency in their life right now and they're really in a hurry to get to the hospital or to get home. I hope everybody's okay.*

Another way to reframe is to use a "loving kindness" meditation. If you're doing that talk again, and people are not answering or not giving their feedback or they're looking in a way that you can easily interpret it as they don't think what you're saying is very smart or effective are worth listening to. Rather than taking it in and focusing it toward yourself like there's something wrong with you, give yourself a "loving kindness" thought. In other words, you think about yourself in a kind way. Think about the people you are speaking to in a kind way, and say to yourself, *I know that everything's going to work out. I wish myself and all of the people here today good health and well-being.* I know this may seem kind of pollyanna-ish but you can't be having positive thoughts and negative feelings at the same time.

There is evidence that shows that having a positive attitude toward others can shift your emotional state to be more positive and can lift you out of the negative feeling states that can accompany limiting beliefs. These are just hacks to get yourself into a more positive frame of mind about anything that's happening.

Cognitive Strategy #2
Challenging Your Thoughts

Another cognitive strategy is to challenge the thoughts that you're having. Let's just say you think everybody thinks that what I'm doing is not good enough, or you think, "I'm never good. I never write about anything. Why do I even bother?" This is what we call black and white thinking. The idea here is to challenge your thinking.

Here are some things you could say to yourself to challenge your habitual negative thoughts. The first step is to verify the thoughts. Ask yourself, is that true? What is the evidence of that? Perhaps you think you're a fraud. You fear that you're going to be seen as a fraud in the eyes of others, or that you don't have what it takes to do a job.

The second step is to challenge these thoughts. Ask yourself, *Is that really true? So what is the evidence that I can't do anything right?* Then ask yourself, *What is the evidence that I can do things right?* Those thoughts might look like this. *You know, you did get this job, people did hire you.* If you're in any kind of a high level job, remind yourself of how many interviews you had to go through to get your job. Remind yourself of all the training that you've had to do to get to be able to do this job. Think of the years of education, the jobs that you've had that gave you the skills to be where you are today. Continue on like that, challenging the automatic negative beliefs about yourself when it comes to work.

When it comes to your personal life you may have similarly negative limiting beliefs. *Nobody likes me. I'm never going to have good friends. I have this boyfriend and he doesn't really love me.*

Step one, challenge that. What is the evidence that your negative thoughts are true? Then what is the evidence that these negative beliefs are not true? When you do this, you start to zoom out and see the bigger picture.

Now reframe. Maybe you're not perfect. Maybe there's things that your boyfriend or your husband doesn't like about you, or things that you do that you know your friends might get annoyed about. That's very possible. But in the bigger picture, I bet you there's a lot of other things about you that they really like and reasons why they love you and are with you.

Places you may see these thoughts can be regarding your worth with your partner, your friends, your family and when thinking about work relationships. It's the same idea with work that you can zoom out. You don't have to be perfect in every way. This helps you to relax a little bit. Get calmer in these situations where you are putting yourself on the line.

Cognitive Strategy #3
Is This How I Would Talk with My Best Friend?

Finally, the third cognitive strategy that we'll look at is when you hear yourself giving yourself negative messages or negative self-talk, ask yourself, *Would I talk like this to my best friend? What would I tell him/her/them about this situation? Is this how I would talk to my daughter or my son?* Take a step back and ask yourself these questions. My guess is that when you do that, you are going to say no, of course not.

Most of my clients say they would never talk in such a negative way to someone they love. Then I ask them why is it that you think it's okay to talk to yourself that way? Why is it that you don't deserve the same kind of respect that you would give toward your friends, your family members? When you put things into this kind of perspective it removes the validity of your negative self-talk and/or of your limiting beliefs. Whatever the reason is, you don't have solid ground to stand on there. This is when you come face to face with your limiting beliefs and realize that they aren't truths. You learned them from someone or from your interpretations of events in your life.

What I'd like you to do is to practice stopping yourself when you realize you are using negative self-talk. Ask *what would I tell my friend, my best friend, if they were telling me about this situation?* Then I want you to tell yourself that same response.

This has to do with putting yourself in somebody else's shoes. It will bring you to your basic beliefs about humanity. We are all deserving, worthy of love and respect. It's not just certain people who get to enjoy that privilege. It's a basic human right.

How to Use these Strategies

These are cognitive strategies that will help you to shift out of the negative self-talk, the limiting beliefs that you have and shift into more empowered feelings about yourself. You deserve to feel just as good about yourself as anyone else does. Again, practice, practice, practice. Think about what the negative self-talk is that you have going on all the time. What are some ways that you can reframe it? What are some ways you can challenge it? What would you tell your best friend if they were talking to themselves that way? Remember, change doesn't happen overnight. It takes time and practice.

Now it's your turn to use the strategies we've gone over here to try reframing your own limiting beliefs. Notice your negative self-talk and try to practice these cognitive strategies. Journal about what you are realizing and learning.

Chapter 10

Diving Deeper into Emotional Intelligence

Emotional intelligence is key to being able to identify and resolve limiting beliefs.[7] Emotional intelligence is crucial because everything that we do, every experience we have, every memory we have, has an emotional component to it. In order to be able to access that and resolve it and move on and develop new beliefs about yourself, you really have to be able to access emotions.

Depending on your upbringing, accessing your emotions can be very difficult. You may not have been taught that it's okay to have emotions or you might have been taught that some emotions were okay, but not every emotion was acceptable. Maybe it wasn't acceptable for you to express sadness? We've all grown up with lots of different messages about being emotional beings. In order to experience our lives most fully, it is crucial that we work on getting comfortable with being an emotional being.

This might require you to relearn what you've been taught and that's one of the main things we're

---

[7] For a deeper exploration of this topic, look at the Resources section at the end of this book.

doing in this book. You have the opportunity to recreate and relearn new thought patterns, new beliefs about yourself. To have emotional intelligence is the pathway to be able to feel better and to feel happier. I would like to even take that a step further, that with emotional intelligence, you can have more joy in your life.

Having emotional intelligence and comfort with being an emotional being, you can experience the feeling of love for yourself and be more able to fully have love in your life with other people. In order to do that, you have to be open to all kinds of emotions. We can't just say, I'm going to open my heart to having joy, but shut down anything that has to do with anger or sadness or fear, or shame. We have to be open to the gamut of emotions that we might have and not be afraid of it.

It's really important that we're able to allow ourselves to have our emotions and to be able to process them, feel them, express them when appropriate, and to move on from them. It's when we don't allow this process to happen that our emotions hold us hostage.

What are Emotions?

Before we start talking more about all the different kinds of emotions. I want to define what an emotion is. It's a reaction to events that are happening in your life. It's usually short lived, as opposed to a mood. Your mood is something that usually lasts longer; it could last hours or days. Mood is different from emotions.

People are often afraid of having an emotion because they think they're going to be stuck in it. But the way emotions actually work when you allow them to come up and be expressed is that they usually come to a peak in your experience of that emotion and then it dissipates. As opposed to a mood which is more stable usually and lasts a longer period of time.

What happens when we resist emotions is we hold them in and we can experience a "damming effect" where it feels like they're all bottled up. Then something will happen that triggers emotions and we just explode. I think that's why we tend to feel like emotions are dangerous because we haven't really been taught how to express our emotions or how to deal with them.

Types of Emotions

There are basic emotions present across cultures: happiness, surprise, anger, sadness, fear, disgust, shame, contempt, pride and amusement.

When we talk about emotions, there's a general consensus that there's a limited number of primary emotions and then there's a blending of those emotions to create all different kinds of emotions that are really more different levels or different combinations. Paul Ekman talks about the basic six emotions, and those are happiness, surprise, anger, sadness, fear, and disgust.[8] He also came up with the additional emotions of shame, contempt, pride, and

---

[8] Ekman, P. (1992b). *Are there basic emotions?* Psychological Review 99, 550–553. doi: 10.1037/0033-295X.99.3.550

amusement. According to him, those are the basic emotions that tend to be present across cultures.

General consensus among theorists is that there is a blending of basic emotions which creates emotions such as surprise, happiness and excitement. In addition to the variety of emotions, emotions are on a continuum. You may be furious, or you might be slightly irritated. Some people talk about not having that continuum, especially when it pertains to sadness or anger, that they tend to go from zero to 100 very quickly. My thoughts about this are that it has to do with how they were raised, what was modeled for them in terms of expressing emotions, and maybe what they're aware of in terms of their own emotions. They may be having beginning signs of emotions, but they're not aware of that. When it reaches a 10 in moments they are blindsided.

Components of an Emotion

That brings me to talking more about what the different components of an emotion are. The subjective component, the physiological component and the expression of the emotion.

There's the **subjective component** where something happens, and you start to have a reaction and it's emotional in nature, and it puts you into a different state of mind as you react to that event. That's why they call it subjective.

The second component of an emotion is your **physiological response to the emotion.** The physiological response to fear could be: your palms sweating, your heart racing, tension in different parts of your body. You tend to have that fight or flight response during which you might have adrenaline going through your body, might feel nauseous, you can't breathe, your extremities might get cold. You have an impulse to probably run or fight. These are all physiological experiences that go along with that emotion of fear.

Those reactions tend to be very similar for people regardless of who they are and where they come from.

Then there's the **expression of the emotion** which could look like: crying, yelling or getting angry, expressing the anger. It could even just be facial expressions that come and that are expressed. Everyone has different comfort levels with expressing or showing their emotions. Tension, you might see hands clenching. Jaws clenching. This could be how an emotion gets expressed.

In review, there are three components of an emotion. Ideally, we want to be able to notice all of these different components as they're happening and be able to figure out the best way in the moment to to express and manage them. Depending on how you were raised, what your family and ethnic culture was, you will experience a varied degree of comfort or discomfort with feeling, expressing and then letting emotions go.

Limiting Beliefs and Emotions

As you are going through and exploring all of these limiting beliefs that you might have, trying to identify where they came from, and trying to transform to more positive, empowering beliefs, you're probably going to start to notice emotions more. When you think about where they came from, there's going to be an emotional component to the memory. When I think back on the memory of being mugged I have an image, a negative thought that emerges - *I'm helpless* - and along with that I start to feel some sadness and fear.

Every memory we have contains an emotion. Sometimes they are positive memories and the emotions feel good. Sometimes the memories could be upsetting and the emotions can be scary.

Let's just try to take a moment and think about a limiting belief you might have had in the past or a limiting belief that you're struggling with in the here and now. Whether it's *I'm not enough* or *I'm not ever gonna be able to do this*, or another one, think about what the emotion is that goes along with that belief.

Sometimes it can be difficult to identify the related emotion. If you can't figure out the emotion, notice where you feel a sensation in your body when you think of those limiting beliefs. Paying attention to what happens in your body gives you a beginning clue to what the emotion is that goes along with it. If you have difficulty identifying your emotions, this is a good way to begin to familiarize yourself with your emotional world.

Another inroad to your emotional world is to pay attention to the negative self-talk you engage in and notice the emotion that gets connected to it or that comes up as a result of it. What you'll see is that if you can start to change that negative self-talk you can also start to shift your emotions that you're feeling and that you have to deal with. If you're always putting yourself down you're not going to have happy feelings, happy emotions, you're going to be feeling sad or shame, disgust, all of those kinds of emotions. If you can shift to a more kind and compassionate stream of self-talk, you will start to have more feelings of happiness, joy and other positive feelings.

Self-Awareness and Compassion

There are some other reasons why it's good to have emotional intelligence. When you think about what you're going through in your life, it's really important to have compassion towards yourself.

The more you can recognize what you're going through and give it a name, labeling the emotion, the more likely it is that you're going to be able to respond to it. You're going to be able to say and/or practice being able to comfort yourself in a certain way or soothe yourself in a certain way. If we don't really understand what we're going through and what is happening to us, we don't really know how to soothe ourselves or what we need. The more awareness of your emotions that you have, the more likely it is that you're going to be able to tailor your response to it.

Another reason that it's really important that we understand emotions, is that when we're doing this kind of healing work, we're looking back on how people treated us, and what our limiting beliefs were as a result. We're doing this work now from this adult perspective.

As you look back on scenarios that happened when you were a child, and perhaps these events involved your parents. It helps to have an emotional intelligence to be able to think about what they were expressing, what life stressors might have been coping with. What emotions do you remember them expressing? This can give you an understanding of what they were going through. It helps you to be able to say wow, they must have been going through something. They were probably feeling depressed or they were angry a lot, or they were sad. Were there times when they were happy? That's really important to be able to recognize also.

Having emotional intelligence also helps us to make sense of what happened to us. You are able to look back and see it wasn't your fault, that your parents were just very unhappy people. You can see that your parents maybe were very stressed and sad or angry at that time with each other. As an adult what we know is that, let's just say our parents are not getting along with each other. That's going to affect their mood. That's going to affect how they treat us. So in looking back and doing healing work we can say it wasn't me, it was really that they were struggling personally. This allows us to have a completely different perspective on what happened to us. Then you will be able to put the responsibility on where it really belongs.

Emotional intelligence is a tool for you in your toolbox to be able to create and maintain positive beliefs about yourself as you go through your life. It allows you to understand the people in your life in the here and now. You can more accurately identify what kinds of emotions they're expressing, and maybe attend to them in a different way. Understanding emotions gives you a language to communicate and cope with emotions: your own and others. This is immensely helpful. It allows for better communication with the people in your life which is the road to healthy relationships. This applies to understanding interactions with people in your personal life as well as on the job.

Many of my clients talk about the interactions they have at work and they express confusion about why the other person treated them the way they did or why they reacted in the manner they did. People often have regrets for how they acted at work or in their personal relationships. When they learn more how to identify their feelings and become more curious about the reactions of other people, they begin to see that there is most likely more going on beneath the surface. When they understand the emotions better it makes more sense to them and it also gives them more direction on how to proceed. The more we see people as emotional beings, the greater our ability to understand and connect with them will be.

Understanding Your Emotions

Go to your journal and explore some of the following prompts.

- Happy, mad, sad, scared, surprised, disgusted... How do you and others you know express these emotions? How does it feel when you or others express these emotions?

- What did you learn when you were growing up, about your own emotions, about expressing them and what would happen when you did this?

- What were the most common emotions that were expressed in your family when you were growing up? Have you continued that pattern in your own life as an adult?

- What emotions do you wish you could access more readily?

- Do you think you are in certain moods most often? Can you explore that topic?

Begin to work on allowing yourself to express your emotions in ways that feel comfortable and safe. You may not necessarily know how to do that. Get help if you need it. If you are close to someone whom you trust, you can explore this topic with them and get support and/or feedback from them.

Section V

Do

*"What I intellectually knew and understood about self-worth
has become more internalized/tangible." - Client*

Chapter 11

Implementation

Now it is time to try to apply the learnings from this book into your daily life. You will need to hold yourself accountable to stay on task with doing this. Our habitual perspectives, reactions and habits are going to attempt to have you forget all you've learned and just continue on the way you've been living your life. This is what we can call self-sabotage.

When you find yourself engaging in those familiar if unrewarding patterns, here is what I suggest.

Thank that part of you that thinks these old behaviors and patterns are helpful to you and tell that part of you *I'm in charge now and I'm going to try some new ways of being. I will keep us safe. You can trust me.* Then bring in a new idea, thought, belief and/or behavior that you know is in your best interest and will help you to reach your current adult goals.

I suggest that you keep the journal you used while reading this book and continue to notate limiting belief behaviors and attitudes and use a skill that I taught to bring in a healthier more rewarding behavior and thought. In doing this, notice how it feels.

This is where emotional intelligence comes in handy. Try to identify the emotions you are experiencing. Ask yourself where the emotion is coming from, what thoughts are connected to it. Then you can use your cognitive strategies or your visualizations to help you manage these experiences and move to a better state of mind.

The more you do this, the more automatic it becomes. Practicing new thoughts and behaviors will create new neural pathways.

In order for this shift to happen you do have to stay intentional in your observations and in creating healthier beliefs and behaviors.

If you do this, you can transform your sense of self and your feelings of self worth. In the next chapter, you will learn from people who have already taken this journey and have grown imm-ensely.

Chapter 12

Celebration

While writing this book, I decided to reach out to my past clients with whom I used this BUILD method in the EMDR work that I did with them. I wanted to get their perspective on how this work helped them to make progress in their lives toward greater self-worth. Below are their stories. I am eternally grateful to them for taking the time to formulate their thoughts and ideas about their experiences working with me and how their lives have changed. I am also grateful to them for their willingness and boldness in sharing their powerful stories.

"My self-esteem has always been low, often immed-iately looking at a situation with the 'glass-half-empty'; always looking for approval. While working with Suzanne we explored the source of my trauma, anxiety and fears, my need to have perfect results, never saying 'no' to someone, always putting others first...I began to face those fears. I learned to understand, what I think I knew, that I am a good person, worthy of the love that was always present in my life. I was confusing the need to do good deeds and look for approval, as the basis for good feelings about myself. As a child and adult, I have been extremely fortunate to be surrounded by loving friends and family. I now understand that it is more than ok to accept the love

for my own self-worth. I have made significant changes in my life, after 40 years moved to a new home and after 20 years, sold and moved from a vacation home within one year. I am challenged by these life changes but am so much better equipped to accept and embrace them."

"I have always felt I am a good, positive and intuitive person, but never had confidence, self-permission of skills to create boundaries to protect myself. What makes me a good person is my need to live and care for others, but I missed the other key component, which is I also need to love and care for myself for the sake of others. I blamed myself for not saving my son, on so many levels. I still go to that thought often, but I am able to move past it with understanding that I am not to blame. EMDR brings up raw emotions and feelings and then somehow understanding. I believe I am still a good person and will move forward working everyday to accept my traumas as lessons. I will try to focus on the positive rather than the negative I cannot change.'

"Night and day. I came in very negative and left with a positive attitude. Not that everything was flowers & butterflies, but I had tools to work on the shitty things life presented. You helped me get rid of my general 'catastrophic anticipatory anxiety.' Prior to working with you I wavered between extreme over-confidence and complete lack of faith in myself. I was quick to judge and quick to dismiss feelings and points-of-views of others. I judged myself for these flaws harshly. After working with you, I have endured long periods of calmness and I find that I am friendlier and more approachable. I work on my flaws without judging myself as harshly as I might have previously."

"I felt I had no self-worth prior to my EMDR sessions with Suzanne as I always thought I was adopted or a mistake. My mother's controlling stayed with me from childhood through adulthood and for years after she passed away. After my work with Suzanne, many people saw a great change in me. I would face people to talk and actually smile. I became sought out by others because my whole vibe, my energy had changed. It was like moth's attracting to a flame. Today...I am living life, my confidence level is at it's peak. I don't get locked into worry mode even if something hasn't happened nor if something does happen, as I'm now able to assess situations and handle them accordingly."

"I always felt I wasn't important. Once people got to know me they wouldn't want anything to do with me. I love history, reading. I don't drink a lot. I just didn't fit in. All of the 'cool kids' who are interested in whatever the latest trend or tv series is would realize who I am and ditch me. After 'our' work together, I realized I don't owe them anything. I have the right to be happy. My family is important. I want to spend time with them. It's not my problem that someone doesn't want to work a Saturday evening shift. My time is too precious. If someone is gaslighting me I do not owe them anything. That is my time and I don't want to hang out with mean, manipulative people."

"I had very little self-worth prior to our meeting. Through EMDR I was able to learn about my negative cognitions that were holding me back from seeing the person I am or I can become."

"At the onset, I was actually feeling pretty good about myself. EMDR helped me to stop being stuck in the past

and to feel safe and confident. It built upon the already positive self-worth that I had gained via Al-Anon."

"I feel (my self-worth) has improved. I feel like it's been improving over the years and our work was a step along the way toward a more whole me. My confidence in making loving and compassionate decisions for family members increased dramatically. As a result, I didn't doubt my judgment nor feel weighed by guilt and uncertainty."

"Before I thought I was the last person that deserved love. Everyone and everything took priority over my own feelings, needs and well-being. I constantly drove myself to the brink of mental, emotional and physical breakdown because I did not believe I was worthy of saving. I felt the need to save everyone else at the expense of myself because I never wanted them to feel abandoned as I had been. I was so consumed with everyone else's needs that my own were lost. I know (now) that I am worthy of compassion and respect and love and so much more. Now the work that remains is to put this into practice in every aspect of my life."

"I blamed myself for everything, wasn't able to have healthy relationships...I learned to appreciate myself and now have an amazing marriage that wouldn't have been possible without EMDR."

"My self-worth was increased, and my anxiety was decreased after we worked together."

"Before working together, I had spent almost a year in a relationship with someone who treated me like dirt. There was no respect and I knew it was bad and that I was unhappy but I stayed. That was until he broke up

with me of course. I had no self-esteem. I was beautiful and only focused on feeling fat (which I wasn't). I didn't have a lot of confidence outside of my job which meant I made everything about work and my personal life was full of distractions and getting drunk. Work, while I liked what I did, I knew I wasn't valued by the company and people I worked for. I feared being fired and asking for more. When looking back I realize just how invaluable I was to them. After pieces of my life starting falling into place in a way I could only explain as being a direct result of the work we did together. I care about feeling good. I look in the mirror and see a beautiful woman. I put on any outfit from my closet and feel comfortable wearing it. I can't be talked down to or pushed around. I won't let myself anymore. When I got my new job, I pushed back on their offer twice! I knew I had value. I got to celebrate that win with you. I'll always struggle with insecurities and doubts but at the end of the day, I'm a really great person and have a lot going for me and nobody can tell me otherwise. You gave me the foundation for that."

As the last client said above, the work I do provides a foundation for all of us to move through our lives with greater awareness and to have choices about how to continue moving forward in our lives.

The key to making lasting changes in our lives is to remain aware and to intentionally choose healthier perspectives. The teachings and tools in this book give you the foundation to take these actions and as a result, to create new beliefs about yourself as well as to make lasting and significant changes in your life.

It takes practice and continual self-correction as you go. In this book you read people's stories of how they begin to slide backward into old beliefs and emotional states. They say that they catch themselves and self-correct. They use their tools and reinforce the healthier and more positive self beliefs. The more you do this, the more your beliefs of worthiness will prevail over your limiting beliefs.

As you look to the future, take some time to reflect about how you can maintain the momentum you may have created while reading this book. If you feel stuck you can always reach out to me to consult about what may be the next step for you.

Another way you can also further integrate this information is my online course, *Feeling Good in Your Life; Breaking Through Limiting Beliefs.*

This and other resources can be found on my website, www. suzannemccollllc.com

Congratulations!

Now, you get to celebrate as well. Congratulations! You have made it through this book and moved through the five-step BUILD Method.

In following this method, you will be on the road to reclaiming your self-worth. You deserve that. We all do. Take a moment to acknowledge yourself for believing in yourself enough to read this book and thoughtfully apply the concepts and techniques in your life. Remember, this is one step in your journey. You can go back over this many times to try to get more out of it and to continue to grow.

Best of luck, be well and know you are worthy.

The Five-Step BUILD Method

B - Believe in your worth.

U -Understand the way we develop our sense of self and beliefs about ourselves.

I - Identify your limiting beliefs that are interfering with you owning your self-worth and how trauma may be having an impact on you.

L- Learn strategies, tools; educate yourself about emotional intelligence.

D- Do, practice all you've learned. Put it into action.

Resources

In the resource section, I am providing you with resources that you may want to look into in order to further explore the topics discussed in this book. This list is by no means exhaustive of the topics and areas of self-growth that are available to us in taking further steps, but in each reading, course, podcast or intensive therapy treatment that you engage, new awareness and personal growth will occur and the next steps will always be there. Your job is to be open to them and say yes to the opportunity to evolve.

EMDR

Baldwin, M., Korn, D. (2021) *Every memory deserves respect: EMDR, The Proven Trauma Therapy with the Power to Heal,* Workman.

Parnell, L. (2008) *Tapping In, A step by step guide to activating your healing resources through bilateral stimulation.* Sounds True.

Shapiro, F. (2012). *Getting past your past: take control of your life with self-help techniques from emdr therapy.* Rodale Books.

Further EMDR Resources and Therapist Listings

Eye Movement and Desensitization and Reprocessing Therapy (EMDR) International Association

https:// www. EMDRIA.org

Emotional Intelligence

David, S. A. (2016). *Emotional Agility*. Penguin Random House.

Goleman, D. (1995). *Emotional intelligence*. Bantam Books.

Brown Brené. (2021). *Atlas of the heart: Mapping meaningful connection and the language of human experience*. Vermilion.

Limiting Beliefs and Mindset

Sandberg, S., & Scovell, N. (2013). *Lean in : Women, work, and the will to lead (First)*. Alfred A. Knopf.

Brown, B. (2022). *The Gifts of Imperfection: 10th Anniversary Edition*. Hazelden.

Trauma

Van der Kolk, B. A. (2015). *The body keeps the score : brain, mind, and body in the healing of trauma*. Penguin Books.

Winfrey, O. (2022). *What happened to you?: Conversations on trauma, resilience, and healing*. Bluebird.

About the Author

Suzanne McColl, LPC, LLC is an EMDR certified Psychotherapist, author, and speaker on resolving limiting beliefs.

Suzanne specializes in helping women from all walks of life resolve limiting beliefs so they can feel confident and empowered in their careers and personal lives. She is passionate about teaching women to connect with their most aligned selves using her knowledge of the human psyche. Suzanne helps women heal from their past traumas to lead them toward a belief in their self-worth and freedom that follows. She works intensively one on one and also provides education and inspiration through speaking, webinars, online courses and workshops.

Suzanne draws on her own experiences of struggling with and resolving her own limiting beliefs to lead a more authentic life, as well as over 25 years of providing transformational psychotherapy for her amazing clients. Suzanne knows that "We are all more than our limiting beliefs."

Suzanne lives on the shore in Connecticut, sees her clients remotely and also runs a psychotherapy center where she supports inspired clinicians to do healing work with clients struggling with healing from trauma and with having more fulfilled lives.

www. suzannemccollllc.com

https://www.facebook.com/suzanne.mccoll.98
https://www.instagram.com/suzannemccolllpc/?hl=en
https://www.linkedin.com/company/suzanne-mccoll-lpc/
https://pin.it/2xAYcnr

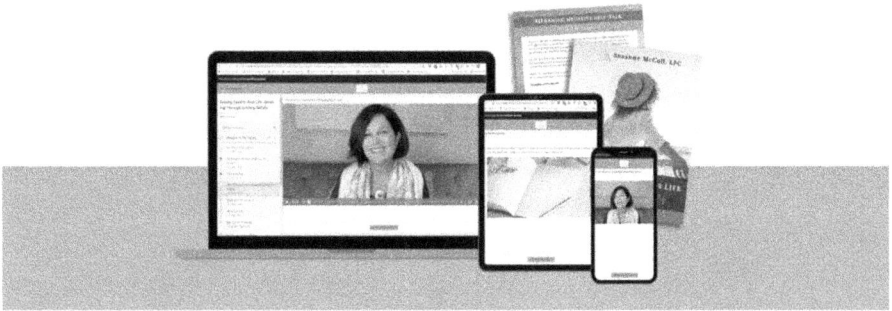

FEELING GOOD IN YOUR LIFE:
OVERCOMING LIMITING BELIEFS

An online course designed to unlock your ability to enjoy a
freer, happier, and more fulfilling life

Register for the course here:

https://suzannemccoll.thinkific.com/courses/feeling-good-in-your-life

About Green Heart Living

Green Heart Living's mission is to make the world a more loving and peaceful place, one person at a time. Green Heart Living Press publishes inspirational books and stories of transformation, making the world a more loving and peaceful place, one book at a time.

Whether you have an idea for an inspirational book and want support through the writing process – or your book is already written and you are looking for a publishing path – Green Heart Living can help you get your book out into the world.

You can meet Green Heart authors on the Green Heart Living YouTube channel and the Green Heart Living Podcast.

www.GreenHeartLiving.com

www.ingramcontent.com/pod-product-compliance
Lightning Source LLC
Chambersburg PA
CBHW072126090426
42739CB00012B/3088